Haunted America

HAUNTED AMERICA

MICHAEL NORMAN
AND
BETH SCOTT

TOR®

A TOM DOHERTY ASSOCIATES BOOK
NEW YORK

This book is dedicated to our families
for always being patient,
and to Mark Lefebvre for never losing faith.

Contents

Foreword
by Michael Norman

There is an awkwardness about seeing my name standing alone above these lines.

Let me explain.

Until her death in February 1994, Beth Scott and I collaborated on a series of books about ghosts and the supernatural, culminating with the work you hold in your hands, *Haunted America*, and its recently published companion volume, *Historic Haunted America*. Sadly, Beth passed away before the hardcover publication of these books.

Our partnership began in the late 1970s, so for all those years I shared a byline with Beth, learning that collaboration means never having to take sole blame—or credit—for what you commit to paper. I guess slicing away half of the byline means I'm now the responsible party, so fire away if you must at this old gray(ing) head!

In the beginning, we had little intention to go beyond our first published effort in 1980, the collection of tales we called *Haunted Wisconsin*. But its popularity has kept it in print over all these years, and led to our writing the first ever compendium of midwestern ghost stories, *Haunted Heartland*, and our final proj-

ects I noted above. Most of this was done with the encourage-
ment of our friend/editor/agent, Mark Lefebvre. Just shows you
what happens when an idea comes along, grabs hold, and won't
let go.

Our philosophy about writing these "true" stories of the supernatural was straightforward from the outset.

We did not want to be ghostbusters and we certainly did not
have the academic credentials to be considered parapsychologists.

We had no desire to prove or disprove any of the stories we
unearthed.

Our approach to the topic was as writers and journalists whose
"beat" happened to be ghosts, hauntings, and the supernatural. In
other words, we were akin to the ink-stained wretches on daily
newspapers everywhere who are ordered by their editors to come
up with the "annual Halloween story."

We wanted to pull together in single collections what we
thought were the most fascinating ghost stories in a particular region or, later, in each state of the Union. However, we tried to
tell them imaginatively while maintaining the authenticity of
each one. In some cases we added details that, while not proven
to have taken place, could have occurred within the context of
the particular story.

Are the stories true that you're about to read in these pages?
As an answer, allow me to quote from our introduction to
Haunted Heartland: "What matters most, we believe, is that
these stories have been *told* by the people involved as if they
were true. The tales are passed along as accounts of what (apparently) happened to ordinary, living people."

That's a bit of a cop-out, true, but remember these are *ghost
stories*, after all. And ghosts rarely leave written records! I trust
that readers will feel free to believe or disbelieve as they so desire. But should you decide to question the reality of these dwell-
ers in the dimension of the supernatural, keep in mind Hamlet's
words from Act I, Scene V:

"There are more things in heaven and earth, Horatio,
 Than are dreamt of in your philosophy."

I think Beth would have been pleased with the books that re-
sulted from our nineteen years of research, and would join me in
acknowledging the assistance of scores of individuals all across

the nation, many of whom are mentioned in the Bibliography. To the other librarians, researchers, correspondents, and friends, far too numerous to mention individually without fear of leaving someone out, thank you on behalf of my great friend and colleague, Beth Scott, and myself.

I hope you enjoy these journeys through supernatural America. Have a . . . pleasant . . . trip!

River Falls, Wisconsin
October 1995

THE UNITED STATES

Arizona

Charlotte's Corner

Army Colonel Roy Strom was asleep in a bedroom of old Carleton House at Fort Huachuca. His wife was out of town for a few days and his daughters had returned to school.

Suddenly a loud crash from somewhere in the house startled him awake. Colonel Strom climbed out of bed and set about trying to locate the source of the disturbance. It didn't take him long. In a daughter's now-vacant room he found an Oriental jewelry box facedown in the middle of the floor. The lacquered box's five drawers were still closed. When he picked it up, the drawers and their contents spilled out onto the floor.

Colonel Strom was puzzled. The jewelry box, which he had bought for his daughters during a tour of duty in the Far East, had been sitting on a fireplace mantel a half-dozen feet from where he found it lying on the floor. How did it get there? It would have been impossible for it to have slid off and landed where he found it.

To this day, Colonel Strom, from 1980 to 1982 the deputy commander of the U.S. Army Intelligence Center and School at Fort Huachuca, calls it the most puzzling incident during his stay at the post's *haunted* Carleton House.

Built as the post hospital in 1880, Carleton House performed that role for only a few years before being turned into housing quarters for officers, an officers' mess, post headquarters, a café, and then a schoolhouse. In more recent years, the house has been the residence of the hospital commander or other officers assigned to the base.

Fort Huachuca itself dates from about 1877 and played an integral role in the Indian wars of the 1870s and 1880s. It served as advance headquarters and supply base in the campaign against Geronimo. Later the Tenth Cavalry, headquartered at Fort Huachuca, joined Gen. John Pershing's punitive 1916 campaign into Mexico to find bandit Pancho Villa. The fort was also home to the four regiments now known collectively as the "Buffalo Soldiers," all African-American army units during the nineteenth and early twentieth centuries.

In 1954, Fort Huachuca became the site for advanced testing of electronic and communications equipment. Today, the fort is the location of the Army Intelligence Center and School and the Army's Information Systems Command. All C130 flight training for NATO forces takes place at the fort, as does some training for the Israeli air force and army.

Carleton House is the oldest building on the base. It was named after Brig. Gen. James H. Carleton, the famed leader of the "California Column" during the Civil War. When the fort was temporarily turned over to the State of Arizona from 1947 to 1951, Carleton House was used as a vacation retreat by Governors Sidney P. Osborn and Dan E. Garvey.

Tales of ghostly apparitions and peculiar incidents have been reported by several of the families who have occupied the house.

"I never believed in ghosts. And I didn't change my mind because of 'Charlotte,'" said General Strom, who has been promoted since his tenure at Fort Huachuca.

It was his wife, Joan Strom, who first attached the name Charlotte to their resident spirit. There seems to be no historical connection between the ghost and anyone named Charlotte, other than it being "a nice 1800s sort of name," Mrs. Strom said. She wanted to be able to call the ghost by name, particularly on those occasions when the family wanted to blame "someone" for mischievous activities in the house. And most people who have observed the haunting believe there is a distinctively feminine quality about the spirit.

On the very first day the Strom family moved in, the house's reputation was_impressed upon them. Several local men were hired to help the moving company unload furniture. One worker in particular seemed jittery. He would carry boxes only to the front door before setting them down. His cohorts were upset with his seeming laziness.

"I'm just not going in there," he told them. "That house is haunted."

On that same day, the Stroms piled boxes in what had been the hospital's morgue, now a bedroom a few steps below the level of the rest of the house. Sometime that evening all the boxes were torn open and the contents strewn about the room.

The family dog was blamed for that piece of mischief, but Roy Strom really isn't convinced it wasn't something else.

A day or so later, Strom was home alone when the doorbell rang. He answered but no one was outside. Twenty minutes later the bell rang again. This time, he checked all four entrances to the house, each with a doorbell, but again didn't find anyone. A few minutes later, the doorbell buzzed again. Strom figured it might be some kids pulling a prank, so he raced around the house trying to catch whoever was out there. Again unsuccessful, Strom arrived at his own solution a half-hour later when the bell rang once more. He disconnected the wiring.

Four chandeliers in the cavernous knotty pine living room, formerly the hospital's ward room, also seem to cause occasional problems. A separate switch controls each pair of lights so that when all four chandeliers are lighted both switches must be flipped on. On the day the Stroms moved in, all four lights worked. But that night Roy Strom found that three of the chandeliers were fine, but a fourth refused to operate. The next morning all four worked fine once again. That pattern was repeated throughout the family's stay at Carleton House when lights suddenly developed sporadic electrical difficulties.

Soon after they moved in, the Stroms hung a number of pictures in the dining room. The adobe walls made the job difficult, but they finished the task after a few false starts. During the night all of the pictures fell down, including a solid-brass Oriental trivet. It was bent nearly in half. Roy tried and failed to straighten it by hand the next day.

"I think I can explain almost everything that happened to us in the house," explains Roy Strom, citing poor wiring for the electrical problems and weak walls for the pictures falling. He still can't understand how the brass trivet became so badly twisted.

Joan Strom sectioned off a portion of the living room which she called "Charlotte's corner." The area is perceptibly colder than the rest of the house (which Roy says is caused by its being close to a stairwell) and the chandelier overhead has always refused to work at night.

Joan thought the ghost was that of a woman who died when the house was a hospital in the 1880s. The woman may have died in childbirth, along with her newborn child. Joan believed that the ghost doesn't think her dead child was properly taken care of or buried. While she lived in the house, Joan searched fort records and a cemetery trying to find evidence of a mother and child's death, but without success. However, records were sketchy during the frontier era, or they may have been lost over the decades. Sometimes those who died were simply buried in unmarked graves.

Two other peculiar events at Carleton House directly involved Joan Strom. Early one morning, she was at a table in the kitchen when she saw her teenage daughter, Amy, walking down an adjacent hallway. Joan called out to her, but Amy didn't stop or return her greeting, which her mother thought very unusual. She got up from her desk and went into her daughter's bedroom. Amy was fast asleep, as were her two sisters. Joan doesn't think it was Amy that she saw in the hallway that morning.

One of the "eeriest experiences of Joan's life," according to Roy Strom, took place one afternoon as she carried freshly washed linen to a bathroom closet. A swirling miasma, a kind of whitish fog enveloped her. Joan said it wasn't hot or cold, dark or damp. It didn't feel like anything, she reported.

Although the legend of the Carleton House haunting has been around for many years, only a few people, perhaps including Joan Strom, have reportedly seen the ghost. One of the first sightings involves the ten-year-old son of a neighbor family who had been sent to deliver a message to the Koenigs, residents of

Carleton House before Roy and Joan Strom. The boy didn't know that the house's front door was actually located at the side. Instead, he went up the front steps and knocked. He later told his parents that Margaret Koenig walked right down the hall toward him but ignored his raps. She had blond hair and wore a long dressing gown.

Puzzled by Mrs. Koenig's actions, the boy's mother later telephoned. Mrs. Koenig insisted she and her family had only just recently returned home. No one had been in the house at the time of the boy's visit. He insisted that a woman *had* been in the hallway of Carleton House.

One of Margaret Koenig's teenage daughters may also have seen Charlotte's ghost. Nancy Koenig had been out late on a date. Earlier that evening, her mother had asked her to "check in" when she returned home. Nancy got home, went into the paneled living room and saw her mother standing at the end of the hallway. "Hi Mom," Nancy called out. "I'm home." She then went to bed. The next morning Mrs. Koenig scolded her daughter for not letting her know when she got home. Nancy insisted she had and described how she had seen her mother in the hall. But it was Charlotte that Nancy may have seen.

Col. Warren Todd, his wife Nancy, and their two sons lived in Carleton House for several years, until 1988. If the Stroms took a somewhat lighthearted view of the house's ghostly reputation, Colonel and Mrs. Todd became reluctant believers that the story of Charlotte may have been something more than a story for the faint of heart.

Warren Todd was the post's hospital commander. He is a pediatrician and mechanical engineer. "I like to look at things and try to make sense out of them," he insists.

Within a month of the family's moving in, Dr. Todd's belief in rational explanations for all events was tested.

"Something happened to the hot water heater," he remembered. The unit was located in a small room under the house reachable through a door near the front steps. "I got a key, went into the room and walked about ten feet before I said, 'I don't like it in here at all.' I never got to the hot water heater. I guess you could say I was 'psyched out.' That room was the only place that I've never wanted to go into. Nothing really happened. I just said that if I didn't have to go in there I wasn't going to."

Dr. Todd said his sense of dread upon entering that isolated cellar was palpable.

According to several psychics who contacted Dr. Todd after the incident was publicized, the little child that Charlotte is said to be looking for may have been buried in that room.

Two key events while the Todds lived at Carleton House convinced them that something else could have been in the house.

The first occurred at about three-thirty one morning while Dr. Todd studied particularly late for a course in health services administration he was taking at the University of Arizona. He sat in the kitchen; the door going into the dining room was shut. A voice that seemed to come from behind the door said, "Father! Father!" Dr. Todd jerked his head toward the sound, concerned that his six-year-old son wanted something. But then he realized that his son never called him "Father," but always "Dad" or "Daddy." He listened for anything further, but went back to his studies after a few minutes of silence thinking that perhaps it was his imagination.

After only a short while, the voice, like that of a child, again called out "Father! Father!" and this time Dr. Todd jumped up from the table, shoved the door open leading into the dining room and raced for his son's room, some twenty feet down the hallway. Little Drew was safely tucked in bed, without any indication that he had been the voice in the night.

The Todds' dog, a dachshund, was never comfortable in Carleton House. He seemed to have a sixth sense that another creature roamed the place, unseen.

Nancy Todd said: "His hackles would go up for no reason at all. We would be in the TV room and he would go racing down the hallway, barking all the time. He dug a hole in the rug at one particular spot in the hallway. There was something about that area he didn't like at all. We finally had to put chicken wire over that part of the carpet. This went on the entire time we had the dog, not just for a few days. He would quiet down for a few hours and then be back at it. There was never anything any of us could see, smell, or hear that would cause him to do that. In the TV room I definitely got the feeling that somebody was standing there, or walking near me."

Interestingly, Nancy Todd didn't feel uncomfortable in the

house. "I was always very secure, even though I don't particularly like being alone. It never felt eerie, and I never wished that I didn't live there."

Nancy also heard a peculiar voice in the house. "I was out on the porch very early one morning, about five. And I heard something. I looked out to see if a jogger or walker was going by but I couldn't see anyone. The only way I can describe what I heard was that it was like a computer-voice, sort of mechanical sounding. It seemed to be saying something like 'Sleep . . . sleep.' "

Her stepson lived with the family during their stay at Fort Huachuca and reported another strange encounter. The boy's bedroom was the one in the lower level, the former hospital morgue.

"He had to cross the front paneled living room, the one with Charlotte's corner, in order to get to his room," Nancy Todd explained. "Well, he had fallen asleep in the TV room and was going back to his bedroom through the living room when he looked to his left and saw a dress. There wasn't any body connected to it, just a long dress that seemed to be standing all by itself."

The boy ran down the steps and "waited for something more to happen. But nothing did," according to Nancy Todd. The next morning he drew a picture of what he had seen: a light-colored gown with ruffled edges around the sleeves and hemline. Just the type of dress a young woman on the Arizona frontier of the 1880s might have worn.

Charlotte's corner of the Todds' living room contained a rocking chair with a baby doll on it. No one ever used the chair. Mrs. Todd thought the chair and doll might help out the ghost on those lonely nights when the "search" for her baby seemed particularly hopeless. "Charlotte is like a young puppy dog," Mrs. Todd said. "She would never do anything with a lot of people in the house."

For his part, Warren Todd doesn't *disbelieve* in ghosts as much as he once did. He actually wanted to "meet" Charlotte, hoping that he could talk to her and find out what she wanted. "If it had not been for that one early-morning episode with the child's voice and with our dog's strange behavior, I would have said it's a cute story but that's all. As a medical doctor and an engineer, I would have to say that Carleton House is worthy of inspection by parapsychologists."

Dead Man's Tree

Three sixth-grade girls in Dover, Delaware, may be the youngest ghost hunters in the country, and possibly the youngest to investigate a haunted governor's mansion. But Michael Castle, former governor of Delaware, believed in the ghostly legends that swirl around the state's official residence, "Woodburn"—an eerie two-hundred-year-old estate—and that is why he agreed to let Holly Forbis, Taryn Morrow, and Faith Truman of the Warner Elementary School of Dover spend the night of May 7, 1985, in the executive mansion.

Accompanied by their teacher, Connie Malin, the youngsters arrived with a Ouija board, a tape recorder, a video camera and monitor, and a stuffed dog to capture the attention of the child ghost who is said to live in the house.

Governor Castle told the group that in January 1985 at his inauguration party at Woodburn, several women guests had complained that something was tugging at their dresses, but when they turned around no one was there. One woman felt that a little girl lingered in a corner of the room, but no one could be seen.

The governor said that in March a second-floor window kept

opening by itself all night and setting off the burglar alarm. Security guards said no one was near the window.

The children were impressed. Perhaps they could solve the mystery. They toured the house and then set up their equipment. By 11:00 P.M. the camera, which had been in perfect working order, wouldn't focus.

"The pictures were clear on the monitor, but you couldn't focus through the lens," the teacher said. "When the girls filmed themselves with the objects they'd brought, they appeared transparent on the monitor, while the props were normal."

The tape recorder failed to operate and the Ouija board yielded nothing.

The equipment failures were especially baffling.

In the morning the girls said they weren't frightened, but were made uneasy by the painting of a woman who they said smiled at them a couple of times as they worked.

Woodburn is Delaware's first executive mansion, purchased by the state in 1966 for $65,000. (Before that time governors provided their own living quarters.) The brick house, on an acre and a half of land on Kings Highway, was built in 1790 by a Charles Hillyard, whose great-grandfather had been given a tract of three thousand acres by William Penn.

On days when the mansion is open to the public, some visitors come to see the exquisite Georgian furnishings, or perhaps sit outdoors by the reflecting pool in the boxwood garden. But many more come in hopes of catching a glimpse of one of Woodburn's four ghosts.

The small girl in a gingham dress apparently shares the house with two others: a gentleman spirit in eighteenth-century garb complete with knee breeches and ruffled blouse drinks wine from a decanter left on a sideboard, and an elderly dinner guest is still trying to find his way to the dining room. Outdoors, close to the house, the ghost of a Southern slave raider inhabits a massive tulip poplar.

Nothing is known about the child ghost, but the others have been authenticated.

In the middle of the nineteenth century the house was occupied by Dr. and Mrs. M. W. Bates. On one occasion Lorenzo Dow, a famous traveling Methodist minister, was a houseguest. As Dow started downstairs to breakfast he was startled to see, on the staircase landing, an elderly gentleman wearing knee breeches, a ruffled shirt, and a white powdered wig. Dow nodded and continued on downstairs. When he reached the breakfast room, Mrs. Bates asked him to lead the family in prayer.

"But shouldn't we wait for your other guest?" said Dow.

"There is no other guest," snapped Mrs. Bates.

Dow was not easily put off and went on to describe the "person" he'd seen.

Mrs. Bates was visibly upset, and after the meal was over, she asked Lorenzo Dow not to relate the incident to anyone. He learned later that the apparition he'd seen bore a strong resemblance to Mrs. Bates's father, who had been dead for many years. Dow was never again entertained at Woodburn.

Although the description of the ghost that Lorenzo Dow saw parallels that of the tippling ghost, who can know if it's the same specter? The late Gov. Charles L. Terry Jr., during whose administration the state bought Woodburn, talked sometimes about a wine-drinking ghost.

"They used to fill bottles of wine for the ghost," Terry told a news reporter, "and in the morning the bottles were empty. One time, a servant swore he saw an old man in colonial costume sitting there in the dining room, slowly drinking wine."

In the 1870s George P. Fisher, a college student, lived in the house. One Christmas he brought a classmate home with him for the holidays. On the first night the two men sat up late swapping stories and making plans for their brief vacation.

At one o'clock they went off to bed—Fisher to his room and the guest to the adjoining room. Before Fisher was undressed he heard a thud in the next room. Throwing open the door between the rooms, he found his friend sprawled unconscious on the floor.

What had happened?

After the man had been revived he told Fisher that he had just entered the room with his candle when he saw, by the dim light, an old man hunched in a chair by the fireplace. To his horror, the man arose and shuffled toward him. The student remembered nothing more. The men searched the room thoroughly and found no evidence of any living thing.

Years later, after George Fisher had become a judge, he enjoyed telling this story. The room his classmate had occupied was the bedroom of Woodburn's builder and first resident, Charles Hillyard. Some believe that Hillyard may have stayed on in the home he loved in life.

The cellar and the Dead Man's Tree command the most interest from visitors. In pre-Civil War days Woodburn was a station on the Underground Railroad. Runaway slaves, trying to escape to the North, were hidden in various cellar rooms, and some of them died there. Is it their death cries that are sometimes heard? Or only the moaning of the wind on a stormy night?

The gnarled old poplar known as the Dead Man's Tree, or Hanging Tree, grows close to the house. Reputed to be more than two hundred years old, it has been split twice by lightning. Legend has it that one night Southern raiders reached Woodburn and attempted to capture the slaves in the cellar to sell them back to their owners. But Daniel Cowgill, the master of Woodburn, drove the raiders off—except for one man who hid in a hollow of the ancient tree. His head somehow became stuck in the hollow and there he died.

Today, children do not loiter while passing Woodburn after dark. They say that you can hear a man groaning inside the tree, and that by the light of a full moon you can see him.

Iowa

Phantoms of the Opera House

On the night of August 15, 1986, Sue Riedel took the stage of Dubuque's exquisite Grand Opera House. The theater was packed for the opening night of *Tintypes*, a musical of George M. Cohan songs from the turn of the century. Riedel welcomed the audience and told them that in 1904 the great Cohan himself had performed on this historic stage during the Grand's heyday as a legitimate theater.

Suddenly, all the lights in the building went out except for those on stage! Electricians hustled along corridors, checking fuse boxes, searching for frayed or broken wires. All seemed in order, but the lights would not come on.

Nevertheless, true to showbiz tradition, the performance went on. If patrons complained about the lack of aisle lights and dark restrooms, their grumblings went unheard. In fact, the thundering applause following the performance assured the Barn Community Theatre that it had found a real home at last. Live theater had returned to Dubuque, to stay.

But with it, some say, came ghostly players who have yet to understand that the curtains have closed forever on their soliloquies.

The community theater company, established in 1971, had performed originally in a barn. Riedel, a speech and drama teacher at Hempstead High School, became artistic director and longed for the day when the troupe could find a permanent home.

Their wish came true in 1986 when a group of dedicated aficionados of live theater bought the Grand Opera House and worked for months renovating it.

Built in 1889–90 at a cost of $65,000, the Grand was known as Dubuque's "temple of the muses," presenting opera, ballet, and minstrel shows, all on a scale rarely seen in the Upper Midwest. The immortal Cohan joined the likes of Sarah Bernhardt, Ethel Barrymore, and Lillian Russell on the list of stars who trod the boards of the Grand.

But with the advent of moving pictures, interest in live theater declined, and in 1928 the beautiful brick and sandstone building became a movie theater. And so it remained for the next thirty-nine years.

By the early 1990s, the Barn Community Theatre was staging eight shows each year in the restored Opera House and rented the building to other groups when its own rehearsals and plays were not in progress.

The Grand is a busy place now, made busier by a complement of ghosts. Or so it is said. Many persons have reported hearing voices on the empty stage, floorboards squeaking when no one walks on them, doors of unoccupied rooms opening and closing, tape recorders turning themselves on, and lights flashing when no one is near the switches.

That electrical problem on *Tintypes'* opening night has never been solved. It wasn't unique. During one production, spotlights rose up and down by themselves, and one particular spotlight kept falling from its batten.

Yet Sue Riedel, for one, oddly enough pays scant attention to this phenomenon. She is often at the Grand until the early morning hours rehearsing lines on the empty stage. She locks up, but when she arrives back the next morning, lights she had turned off are aglow. She knows very well that no one else has been in the building, so her cheery "Good Morning!" to the empty auditorium seems directed toward her unseen companions.

When the Barn Community Theatre first moved into the

Grand, company members found a "ghost light" in the attic. They described it as a lamp with a bare bulb on top that was set on the stage at night to light the theater for "whatever" may be there. Historically, members said, the lamp was left burning because people thought that without illumination they saw "things."

"Theater people are very, very superstitious," Riedel cautioned. Had ghostly thespians "retired" to the attic of the Grand, taking their light with them? Although the lamp has been removed and the attic is used for costume storage, "presences" from the past tarry in the old theater.

Here, then, are a few of the stories told by persons who believe they've brushed against "another world" at the Grand Opera House.

Helen Johnston, a retired teacher, is the office manager of the Grand. She works nine to five Monday through Friday and is often the first person in the building. One morning in 1986, shortly after the Barn players took over the building, Johnston was walking upstairs to her office when she heard noises on the stage.

"I looked to see who was down there," she remembers. "It was very dark, but still I could see that nobody was there. It wasn't a scary feeling, and I'm not a brave person. I really don't know why I wasn't scared. The office is at the back of the balcony and when I got out there the voices were gone. Two years later, I had the same experience."

Johnston is also the theater's accompanist. Her piano is in the orchestra pit, but is moved onto the stage occasionally for a production. And that's where Johnston is most uncomfortable.

"I just feel that there's a presence behind me whenever I play up there," she said.

Sue Lynch-Huerta, like Helen Johnston, has heard disembodied voices in the vicinity of the office. Early one morning she went up there to catch up on some paperwork.

"When I got to the office door," she began, "I heard all these voices and I thought there was a board meeting going on. The voices were predominantly male, but I couldn't make out any words. I knocked and nobody answered so I walked in. Empty.

"Then I heard the voices coming from the stage. I went out

onto the balcony and hollered, 'Hello! Who's there?' I flipped on the lights. Nobody was around.

"After that experience, I decided to talk to the ghosts. I tell them, 'Hello, it's me again. I'm just here to do some work in the office.' I'm never frightened. It isn't as if your hair stands on end and you feel terrible vibes coming at you. But then, I grew up in a 150-year-old house where things moved in the night all by themselves. I guess you might say I'm used to it. I don't think the ghosts are hostile. I think they're happy souls who found a place they enjoyed so much they decided to stay."

Anyone who has built a stage set appreciates the difficult assignment craftsmen in this line of work have, and doubly so when a cold wind heralds a ghost's arrival. Bill Stark, the set builder at the Grand Opera House, volunteers his time, but whenever that cold air tickles his skin he tells his coworkers, "I'm leaving right now. They're here again!"

Stark isn't sure who "they" are, but he knows he doesn't like to be distracted from his work. He always returns later to finish the job at hand.

Sometimes it doesn't even take a chilly breeze to tell Stark that something's amiss. For instance, during a rehearsal of *The Follies*, Stark was upstairs making a videotape of the performance.

"My camera suddenly went haywire," he said, "focusing in and out real fast and real blurry."

Stark went downstairs and found, to his surprise, that a woman was also taping the show and she was having the same problem he was having.

"I'm upstairs and she's downstairs," he went on. "Neither one of us knew that the other was taping."

Although Stark quit taping after his camera malfunctioned, he claims that a picture of a "ghost" appeared on a section of the videotape before the camera troubles. He said it made "a believer out of one guy who never believed in ghosts."

Stark recalled that on another night during the run of *The Follies*, its director from Minneapolis had a run-in with an errant light switch. "One night she and several others turned the lights out, and when they got to the door and turned around the lights were on. It happened twice so the third time she said,

'We're going to turn these lights out and we're going, regardless.' So that's what they did."

The next night the last group out reached to switch off the lights but they went off by themselves. Seems to happen all the time at the Grand Opera House.

Jim Meyer has been associated with Sue Riedel since the early days of the Barn Community Theatre. He calls himself a "jack of all trades," filling in as a company dancer, running the popcorn concession, ushering, taking tickets, even cleaning the theater. When a job needs doing, Meyer is there to do it. He, too, has had some perplexing experiences, especially his first one. It was plain frightening.

"I was painting the front drop with my back to the auditorium," he said. "I was alone. Suddenly, I heard beads clanking. It sounded like a nun walking across the stage. You know how in Catholic schools you can hear the nuns coming a mile away by those beads? Well, I turned to look and as I did I got a blast of cold air. Every hair on my arm and head stood right on end. Well, I put the lid on the paint can and walked out the door and locked it. I was still holding the wet paint brush! I cleaned it at home."

Meyer's account dates to 1986, the year the Barn Players moved into the Grand. He didn't know anything about ghosts then. Within a year, however, he would have another strange encounter.

"Just before Christmas of 1987, I was in the lobby putting up Christmas decorations. I was on one side of the lobby. All my boxes were on the floor on the other side by the ticket booth. I was up on a ladder hanging a wreath and something shoved a box. It went all the way across the lobby."

Meyer shouted, "Knock it off! I haven't got time to deal with you now."

There were no more tricks, and Meyer finished his decorating.

Cathy Breitbach began choreographing musicals for the Barn back in 1988.

"I kind of laughed," she said of the stories she heard about the haunted theater. "I don't believe in ghosts."

Yet the day came when she wasn't so sure.

"We were onstage rehearsing *Gypsy*," she said, "and were well into all the dances. Now my music tapes are never where they're supposed to be. I always have to rewind and find the right song because I've often got ten numbers on one tape.

"Everybody was lined up onstage and we were ready to go. I walked over to my tape recorder to rewind it ... but it turned on—and right to the song we needed.

"I'll never forget that. I thought at first the knob on the machine was loose from all the jumping onstage, but that wouldn't have moved the tape to the exact song that we were doing."

Breitbach said the machine has never since malfunctioned. And she has second thoughts about ghosts.

Jeff Schneider is a newcomer to Dubuque and a novice actor. He said he is also a psychic. In December 1990, he and a friend were doing a photo session at the Grand.

"When we finished," Schneider said, "I felt like someone was standing right behind me. I turned around and saw a man about five feet seven inches tall with orange-colored hair. At the same time I heard the name 'David.' I knew he wasn't a living person. I figured he'd been part of the theater at one time, maybe an actor. But I didn't have any problems with him; he didn't scare me." Schneider would see "David" several times over the coming months.

In January 1991, during a rehearsal for *Anything Goes*, Schneider said he caught glimpses of people in the back of the theater, although no one was out there.

"They appeared like little flashes. I remember an older man with white hair and a white beard stood behind the last row of seats. He wore a tux. I don't know who he was. Although I wasn't really frightened, he kind of bothered me. I wasn't comfortable with him."

Schneider also "saw" two women, one in her thirties and one in her forties, in rear seats with a young man about thirty. They seemed to be attired in old-fashioned clothing. Schneider thinks they are part of the "spiritual residue" that he says is "all over the place."

"The energy here is really strong," Schneider emphasizes. "You can feel it when you walk in. You *know* that there is something here in this theater."

* * *

Even some who have no direct connection to the Grand agree that mysteries abound in the great edifice at 135 Eighth Street.

In the early afternoon of February 10, 1988, businessman Dick Landis stopped by the theater to buy tickets for *Gypsy*.

"The lobby was empty," he recalls, "or at least it was empty to the human eye. I looked behind the ticket counter, but no one was there so I turned to leave. At that moment, the door between the hall and the ticket counter slowly closed and latched. Then, after a few seconds, the door between the hall and the lobby opened, paused, and went partially shut again. I have to wonder if I was truly alone in the lobby."

A Dubuque attorney who prefers to remain anonymous had a similar experience. He entered the theater late one night and saw the concession stand door open and close. Feeling certain that someone was in the building, he went home and got his dog. The pair returned to the theater and searched it top to bottom. They turned up nothing tangible.

Sue Riedel herself recalls an incident that took place during a rehearsal for a children's play one summer.

"One of the little girls said to me, 'Who rehearses before our group? I heard singing on the stage when I came in but I didn't see anybody.' "

Riedel calmly assured the child that it must have been some other group using the theater. In fact, the children's play was the *only* show being rehearsed at the time.

The Dubuque Police Department gets few reports today that something "funny" is going on at the Grand Opera House, but it was not always so. When the building housed a movie theater, cleaning women sometimes called the cops when they heard voices as they went about their nightly chores. Police sweeps never found the source.

Today, the Barn Players accept their haunted theater with a certain nonchalance. "We love our ghosts," says director Sue Riedel. "They don't do anything scary. They don't make things fly around. We just hear them and see things that have happened as a result of them."

Truly, they are the unseen phantoms of the opera house.

Mainely Ghosts

Nell Hilton is the oldest ghost in Maine.

Born before the Revolutionary War, young Nell marched to the beat of her own drummer. She soon grew to resent the strict, Puritan atmosphere of Plymouth, Massachusetts, in which she was raised. In 1740 she persuaded her father to move to Jonesboro, Maine. There Nell found the unfettered life she craved, romping through the woods and making friends with the Passamaquoddy Indians.

But one night Nell's father found his vivacious daughter making love to a Passamaquoddy brave, and in one glancing blow, dispatched him with a hatchet. Despite Nell's frantic screams, Mr. Hilton scalped the interloper.

With her lover dead, Nell turned on her father, crying that he had just killed the man she was to marry. Mr. Hilton ordered her out of his house. "You can spend the rest of your life with them," he shouted. And that's just what Nell Hilton did.

For the next thirty-five years, Nell succeeded in living between two worlds. She made friends with Indians living in French Canada and the American colonies. She often acted as a translator for the French traders who dealt with the Passama-

quoddy and other tribes. There is even some evidence that Nell
was a schoolteacher in New Brunswick and Maine.

Nell's special gift, however, the one that gives her a noted
place in Maine folklore, was her ability to foretell war. After the
French Acadians were driven from Nova Scotia by the British in
1755, legend has it that Nell correctly foretold the war that followed. She advised the Indians to remain loyal to the French.
They apparently showed more honesty toward the Indians than
did their British adversaries.

The next twenty years of Nell's life are obscure. She apparently resurfaced in her old hometown of Jonesboro sometime in
1775. Tensions that would erupt in the Revolutionary War a year
later were already simmering. She is said to have warned the
townspeople that war was imminent, outlining what would become the Battle of Lexington and the eventual Patriot victory
that culminated in the British surrender at Yorktown.

Nell Hilton would not live to see that happen. She was cap-
tured by the British in 1777. Because of her French and Patriot
sympathies years before, the Tories had enough "evidence" to
convict her as a spy. She was hanged at St. John, New Brunswick, on March 1, 1777.

As she stood on the gallows, she vowed to return on the an-
niversary of her death at the "prophecy rock" near Hilton's Neck
whenever war threatened America. It's said that her ghost re-
appeared prior to the War of 1812, the Mexican conflict of 1846,
in 1861 before the Civil War, and then preceding the Spanish-
American War of 1898 and World War I. Nothing is known
about her appearances before World War II, Korea, and Vietnam.
And no one apparently saw her March 1, 1990, ten months before Operation Desert Storm in the Persian Gulf..

Perhaps even ghosts become tired of war.

A Remarkable Monument

Col. Jonathan Buck was many things. Patriot. Magistrate. Pro-
genitor of an old Maine family. Founder of Bucksport. By most
accounts he was a moral, straightforward man often called upon
to settle disputes of varying severity.

But did he also have an evil side? Did this man known for his probity once send an innocent person to the gallows? And could this mistaken death have produced a curse whose effects are visible to this day?

These questions are at the center of a controversy over just what produced this peculiar, leg-shaped outline on Colonel Buck's monument in a cemetery near the town he founded, Bucksport, Maine. Nearly fifteen feet high, the granite obelisk is clearly visible along U.S. Highway 1, about eighteen miles south of Bangor. The name "Buck" is etched on the front. An inscription on the side reads:

COL. JONATHAN BUCK
THE FOUNDER OF BUCKSPORT
A.D. 1762
BORN IN HAVERHILL, MASS. 1719
DIED MARCH 18, 1795

Soon after the monument was erected by Colonel Buck's descendants in 1852, what seemed to be the contours of a human leg appeared just below the name "Buck." Despite repeated attempts to excise the image, it remains vivid to all who visit the cemetery.

The truth behind the "witch's curse," as local townspeople call the legacy of Jonathan Buck, is wrapped in mystery and legend. The various tellings of the tale vary with the speaker or writer. Some are in agreement as to basic facts, while others are wildly divergent from what is known about the life of Colonel Buck. All constitute one of the most fascinating of all Maine traditions. What follows is an attempt to recount the most prevalent myths to see how they square with the probable truth.

Colonel Buck was born in Massachusetts, though not at Haverhill as the monument states. He gained his military title in the Revolutionary War and moved to Maine sometime late in the eighteenth century. One version of the Buck legend draws upon his early Massachusetts life:

A woman had been accused as a witch and Colonel Buck was asked to preside at her trial, a rapid affair in which the defendant was presumed guilty and quickly condemned to death. Before she was hanged, however, the woman looked at Colonel Buck and placed a curse on him. A newspaper account from 1899 recounting the Buck legend had the woman uttering these words: "Over your grave they will erect a stone that all may know where your bones are crumbling into dust ... upon that stone the imprint of my feet will appear and for all time ... will the people from far and near know that you murdered a woman. Remember well, Jonathan Buck, remember well. ..."

This "witch's curse" is the most popular form of the Buck legend. However, there is no record of a witch being executed in Maine. Even in Massachusetts, where Colonel Buck was born and lived for many years, the last of the infamous witch trials took place nearly thirty years before his birth.

Another version, alternately placed in Massachusetts and Maine, provides another connection between a human leg and Colonel Buck:

It seems that Colonel Buck—called "Judge" Buck in this account—was a severe and unforgiving administrator of justice. The grisly remains of a woman were found near town. One of her legs had been neatly sawn off. Under pressure from alarmed townsfolk, Buck hauled in a "suspect," a mentally impaired hermit who lived in a shack at the edge of town. He was given a perfunctory trial and sentenced to death. The recluse looked at Buck and swore that the image of the dead woman's missing leg would appear on Buck's tombstone as a sign of this miscarriage of justice.

This, too, doesn't quite fit the facts of the case. Colonel Buck was only a justice of the peace and did not have the power to condemn anyone to death. No historical record exists to show that he was a judge in Massachusetts before moving to Maine.

In 1913, Oscar Heath, a former resident of Bucksport, wrote a sensational version of the story called "Jonathan Buck, His Curse." Heath added a new twist to the old tale. His story was "narrated" by the *son* of the "witch." The accused was not hanged, Heath wrote, but rather burned at the stake. The child witnessed his mother's horrible death, including the gruesome sight of her burning legs falling off her torso. He grabbed one of her charred limbs and struck Colonel Buck with it.

Poet Robert P. Tristram Coffin added to the Buck legend in a 1939 verse titled "The Foot of Tucksport," a thinly disguised reference to Bucksport. Coffin's main character was "Colonel Jonathan Jethro Tuck."

A boy, the witch's son, also figures prominently in Coffin's poem. The woman accuses "Colonel Tuck" of fathering her child. No crime is committed by her, but rather it is the intolerant townspeople who fall upon the hapless woman and drag her away after she shouts her accusations against the colonel in the town square:

> They dragged the crone to her poor hut,
> They tied her to her door,
> They brought and heaped the withered boughs,
> Against the rags she wore.
>
> The thunderhead touched on the sun,
> And a shadow came,
> Just as Colonel Tuck bent down
> And touched the boughs with flame.

Coffin has the dying woman condemning the colonel with her last breath:

> "And so long as a monument
> Marks a grave of thine
> So long shall my curse inscribe
> Thy tombstone with my sign!"

Folklore and sensationalism aside, is there any truth to the witch's curse of Jonathan Buck? Or is he just the victim of a bad press?

Colonel Buck apparently was highly moral, with a clear sense of right and wrong. A stern man, many would say. He was respected by his neighbors for his military exploits. His election as justice of the peace was doubtless a result of the high esteem in which he was held.

Could there have been the proverbial skeleton in Buck's closet? It's possible. Though he was never formally selected as a judge in Massachusetts, it's conceivable that in the absence of proper authorities in the region he was asked to preside at a trial by virtue of his military rank. Who knows what may have happened? Perhaps he did confront someone accused of witchcraft, or other heinous acts, and did participate in that person's execution.

What cannot be disputed is the eerie outline of a human leg on Colonel Buck's monument a few feet from his final resting place. Most of the curses have the leg showing up on Buck's actual tombstone, but this seems to be a small error. After all, what is a few feet for a curse that is two hundred years old?

As long as the monument stands, passersby will look and wonder if the late Col. Jonathan Buck is still plagued by a witch's last words.

Cyrus

Cyrus was the night clerk for many years at the historic Kennebunk Inn. He was an elderly gent, quiet and conscientious, who could often be found at his desk in a room behind what is now the hotel's bar. Cyrus's life was devoid of eccentricities. Now that he's dead, however, Cyrus could be making up for all of that. His ghost may be the cause of mischief sometimes reported at the inn.

Built as a private home in 1791, the three-story, clapboard Federal-Victorian building changed hands several times before its conversion to an inn called "The Tavern" in the late 1920s. The inn was expanded to sixteen rooms in 1940 by Walter Day and renamed the Kennebunk Inn. During this era Cyrus was employed by Mr. Day.

Arthur LeBlanc bought the place in 1980, added a half-dozen rooms, and passed the word that the old lodge was haunted.

According to writer Robert Ellis Cahill, "Cyrus" was a nickname first given to the resident ghost by a waitress, Pattie Farnsworth. In bringing up supplies from a food locker in the cellar one day, she told owner LeBlanc that the name "Cyrus" came to her. She said he lived under an unfinished set of steps that led from the cellar floor to the ceiling.

The ghost made himself known in distressing ways. A waitress carrying a tray of stemware saw one of the glasses rise several inches into the air and crash to the floor. Several diners witnessed the incident. The waitress took the rest of the day off.

A bartender named Dudley also encountered Cyrus. Late one August evening, a German, hand-carved wooden mug sailed from a shelf behind the bar and struck Dudley on the side of his head. A lump on the barkeep's skull seemed to support his allegation, according to those who spoke with him later.

Angela LeBlanc, the owner's wife, found out quite by accident that waitress Pattie Farnsworth's intuition about their ghost's name was prescient. One day as the LeBlancs and several friends were discussing Cyrus's recent antics, a stranger showed up at the bar. Apologizing for intruding, he asked if Cyrus was still around. He was the resident ghost, Arthur LeBlanc explained. The elderly visitor shook his head. He said he'd lived at the inn as a young man just prior to World War II and Cyrus was the night clerk at that time. In fact, he continued, Cyrus had his desk in a room directly above the basement's unfinished staircase!

Coincidence? Or evidence of a haunting?

Cahill, an author and collector of Maine ghost stories, tried to discover the truth when he stayed at the inn with three friends. Although Cahill didn't hear or see anything, one of his companions asleep in the same room was kept awake by a raspy, moaning voice. Another of Cahill's friends wanted to use the bathroom in the early morning hours. He changed his mind when a chilling breeze enveloped his legs as soon as he stepped out of bed.

Yet the man assigned to stay in Cyrus's old room didn't feel or hear anything unusual.

In nearby Kennebunkport, former president George Bush's occasional vacation home, the picturesque Captain Lord Mansion Inn harbors quite a different specter.

In 1978, a young bride on her honeymoon was understandably upset when a woman attired in a nightgown glided across her bedroom suite and vanished.

Despite some effort, no one has been able to explain who the intruder might have been, or why she was still hanging around the inn.

Windham's Ghost Tower

In the village of South Windham, a few miles southeast of Sebago Lake, a poltergeist is said to ring a bell even though it is no longer there to be rung!

The house on Windham Center Road originally belonged to the Gould family—famous as statesmen and writers. Near the house is a large outbuilding, open on the ground floor so that farm equipment could be easily driven under cover. There is an enclosed second floor for storage and, in one corner, a tower juts heavenward.

On the second floor, and in the tower, footsteps are sometimes heard skittering across the squeaking floorboards. According to legend, the bell that was once housed in the tower was used to sound alarms in the War of 1812 and for raids during the Indian wars.

Whoever the ghost might be, his warnings have long since ceased to cause alarm in neighborhood residents.

Ordinary People

James M. Herrmann and his wife, Lucille, were a hardworking couple with two youngsters. In 1958, they lived in a well-kept green ranch home in Seaford, Long Island, with their two children—twelve-year-old Jimmy and a thirteen-year-old daughter, also named Lucille.

Mr. Herrmann, an Air France employee, commuted the thirty-five miles daily to his work in New York City. His wife, a registered nurse, stayed home to care for the family. Pleasant, kindly folks. But you wouldn't have wanted to visit them. Not in Seaford. Not in the late winter of 1958 when frightening, inexplicable events bedeviled the Herrmanns for five weeks—events that neither the police nor the country's most prestigious parapsychologists were able to explain.

The disturbances began on the afternoon of February 3, 1958. Mrs. Herrmann and the children were home alone when they heard the unmistakable sound of bottles popping their caps. The sounds came from all over the house. In the cellar a gallon bottle of bleach and a can of paint thinner were found uncapped, the contents spilling across the cement floor.

Up in the kitchen, they found that a bottle of starch under the sink was on its side, its cap off and the sticky, blue liquid dribbling onto the linoleum. In the master bedroom, Mrs. Herrmann discovered a small bottle of holy water tipped over. The cap was unscrewed and the water ran across the dresser top. Mrs. Herrmann, a devout Catholic, was greatly upset.

Next to the master bedroom, in Jimmy's room, legs were broken off a ceramic doll and pieces had been chipped from a plastic ship model.

When James Herrmann arrived home, he didn't know what to make of his family's incredible stories. But he warned each of them to say nothing to anyone.

On Sunday morning, February 9, the whole family was gathered in the dining room when the popping noises occurred again. James rushed from room to room. Holy water, toilet water, starch, bleach, paint thinners—the same bottles of liquid opened again by some force. In the bathroom a bottle of shampoo and a bottle of medicine had somehow dumped their contents into the sink.

James called the police. Patrolman J. Hughes was dispatched to the house. While he and the family sat in the living room the popping noises began again in the bathroom. Officer Hughes hurried into the empty room. The shampoo and medicine bottles were again upset. The officer would write later in his report that no appliances were running at the time, the house was quiet, and there were no obvious vibrations or outside noises.

After Officer Hughes made his preliminary findings, Detective Joseph Tozzi was assigned full-time to the case. He ordered a number of tests. An oscillograph used for measuring the slightest vibration was put in the basement. One bleach bottle spilled, but no vibrations in the floor were associated with the incident. The liquid was analyzed at the police laboratory; no foreign matter or signs of manipulation were found.

The Long Island Lighting Company checked all the wiring, fuse boxes, and ground wires in the house and found them in good working order. Maps of the terrain beneath the house showed no underground springs, and inspectors from the Town of Hempstead Building Department pronounced the house structurally sound, with only hairline cracks in the basement floor, probably caused by settling.

The Seaford Fire Department inspected a well in front of the house to see if any change in water level could have caused tremors felt inside the house. They determined that the water level had been stable for the previous five years.

Thinking that high-frequency radio waves might be causing the damage, Detective Tozzi interviewed a neighbor who had a radio transmitter. But the man said he hadn't used his set for a number of years.

Mitchell Airfield was contacted for a list of planes leaving on a runway near the Herrmann house on the theory that airplanes taking off *might* correlate with disturbances within the house. There was no correlation.

A layperson suggested capping the chimney to prevent downdrafts. This was done. It solved nothing.

A Roman Catholic priest also came, on request, to bless the house. But the bottles kept popping with such regularity that the media, by this time, were headlining the story. Press, radio, and television coverage was extensive. And letters from crackpots and publicity-seekers from all over the world deluged the mystified family with advice. The little town of Seaford had never experienced such notoriety.

But now, with the apparent elimination of natural causes for the disturbances, how could one interpret them? People said pranksters were at work, and some attention was focused on twelve-year-old Jimmy Herrmann.

The boy was a bright, brown-eyed honor student at the Seaford Junior-Senior High School who did exceptionally well in English and math. His hobbies were airplane and railroad lore, about which he was unusually knowledgeable. He also read science-fiction books, collected stamps, and enjoyed drawing pictures of rockets.

An obviously gifted child, he was clearly a joy to his parents, and well liked by teachers, friends, and neighbors. A not atypical preteen. Although the boy was not always in the room when the various destructive acts took place, he was usually somewhere in the house.

On Saturday, February 15, 1958, Miss Marie Murtha, a middle-aged cousin of James Herrmann, arrived for a visit. At one point during the day she sat on a chair in the living room while Jimmy sat across from her in the middle of the couch with his arms folded. His sister, at the far end of the room, was the only other person present.

Suddenly a porcelain figure flew off the end table at one end of the couch and fell to the living room rug, but did not break. Miss Murtha couldn't explain the incident, but she told investigators later that she didn't think anything "supernatural" was involved.

On February 20 the mysterious forces struck with renewed vigor. Twice the porcelain figurine was thrown ten feet across the living room, the last time smashing it. A bottle of ink from a writing desk hurtled through the air, splattering the living room rug and wall. And a sugar bowl danced on the dinette table, then fell to the floor.

James Herrmann was devastated. His was a close-knit, affectionate family. He was certain his children were *not* playing tricks, that some agent he could not understand was accountable for wrecking havoc upon his lovely home.

The next day, James moved his family to the home of friends for a few days. Their sleep was blissful, uninterrupted. And when they returned to their own home, peace also prevailed. No bottles lost their caps and no objects levitated and crashed into the walls. Everything seemed normal. For a while.

On the night of February 25, a ten-pound portable phonograph in the basement reportedly flew several feet through the air and crashed against a shelf. An eighteen-inch statue of the Virgin Mary sailed from a dresser top and hit a mirror on the opposite wall. Oddly, neither one broke. And a moment later, a radio fell from a table and skittered across the floor.

Two nights later, *Newsday* reporter Dave Kahn visited the house. He was there to observe and write about a "typical" night in the Herrmann home. His most amazing moments came as he sat reading in the living room. By glancing up, he could keep his eyes on a direct line with Jimmy's open bedroom door. Without warning, a ten-inch world globe, kept on the top of a steel bookcase in the boy's room, soared through the doorway, crossed the hallway, and landed on the living room floor close to Kahn's feet. The reporter rushed into the bedroom and found Jimmy sitting up in bed rubbing sleep from his eyes. Blankets covered his legs. The tall bookcase had toppled over and was wedged between one corner of the bed and a radiator. Jimmy said the noises had awakened him.

Kahn wrote that it was "possible but improbable" that the boy had thrown the globe.

Others would witness equally puzzling events.

A week after Kahn's visit, John Gold, New York correspondent for the *London Evening News*, visited the Herrmanns. He claimed to have seen a flashbulb rise slowly from a table in the living room and strike a wall some four yards away.

In the late afternoon of that same day, four sharp knocks came from the kitchen wall.

And in the dining room a heavy glass centerpiece flew from the table and hit a cupboard, chipping a piece of molding from the cupboard before falling to the floor. Mrs. Lucille Herrmann told Gold that it was the second time that the centerpiece had moved by itself.

Mrs. Herrmann also found an expensive new coffee table flipped over. Such force had been exerted that the table was damaged. She asked Detective Tozzi and an associate, Sergeant Reddy, to come over and emotionally told them that the destruction in her home had to stop, even if it meant calling in a psychic or spiritualist medium. However, Mrs. Herrmann insisted the events were *not* supernatural in origin.

She didn't have to resort to that. In early March, the Herrmanns received a letter from Dr. J. B. Rhine, then director of Duke University's famous Parapsychology Laboratory in Durham, North Carolina. He and his colleagues had been studying the press accounts of the case and believed it merited their attention. The laboratory was investigating such phenomena as telepathy, clairvoyance, precognition, and psychokinesis. Because of the presence of youngsters in the family, Dr. Rhine gave some consideration to the possibility of a poltergeist at work. That phenomenon is usually found in homes where young children or teenagers are present. Although it's never been proven, the theory is that when sexual energies build up in teenagers those energies *may* be transferred into a sort of "vibration" that leaves the body like a radio impulse and plays havoc wherever it hits. Dr. Rhine asked permission for his colleague, Dr. J. Gaither Pratt, to visit the family.

Dr. Pratt was welcomed. He told the Herrmanns that, although reports of incidents similar to those they were experiencing were fairly common, none had been authenticated to the satisfaction of scientists.

Shortly after Dr. Pratt arrived in Seaford, he summoned a

research colleague, William G. Roll, to join him. Both investigators interviewed family members individually and were convinced that none of them was perpetrating any prank.

"The family was much too shaken for it to be a colossal hoax," Dr. Pratt told a United Press reporter. Mrs. Herrmann also lived in constant fear that a flying object might injure someone.

On the night of March 10, 1958, at 8:14 P.M., while Mrs. Herrmann, Jimmy, and Lucille were preparing for bed (James Herrmann was away), the parapsychologists heard a popping noise in the cellar. Dr. Pratt hurried downstairs. A bleach bottle in a cardboard box had lost its cap. The bottle rested against one side of the box, with its cap behind the box.

Both investigators wanted to discover if this particular phenomenon could be achieved by known physical forces, and they began to experiment.

Roll detailed their findings in his book, *The Poltergeist*:

On the theory that someone in the home had surreptitiously placed a chemical in the bottles that would generate pressure, or that pressure had arisen in some other way, we bought some pieces of dry ice, that is, carbon dioxide in its solid state, and placed these in containers with screw caps, such as those in the Herrmann household. We found that when the top was loosely screwed on, the pressure easily escaped with a low, hissing noise without affecting the cap. When we screwed the cap on as tightly as we could by hand, the pressure increased until the gas forced its way out around the threads of the cap but without perceptively loosening it. Of course, thousands of housewives every year do pressure canning in glass jars utilizing this principle—without complaining of "bottle poppings." Pressure escapes from the tightly closed lids without causing them to unscrew. When Gaither and I tightened the cover mechanically, we succeeded in exploding a bottle of relatively thin glass, but the cap remained on the broken neck. This had never been observed in connection with the bottles that lost their caps in the Herrmann household. When we used a bleach bottle of the type which had lost its cap when we were in the house, and when we tightened the cover mechanically, the buildup of pressure inside the bottle produced neither explosion nor unscrewing of the cap. In general, it became clear that pressure does not cause these types of caps to unscrew and come completely off. Either the gas escapes around the threads or the bottle explodes, the cap remaining in place. We found it made no difference if we oiled the threads of the glass.

For inexplicable reasons, this March 10 bottle popping was the last act of the Seaford "poltergeist," if, indeed, that is what it was. There had been a total of sixty-seven recorded disturbances between February 3 and March 10, a period of just thirty-five days. Incredibly, the Herrmanns had been visited by detectives, building inspectors, electricians, firemen, plumbers, parapsychologists, and various other "experts." None had offered a satisfactory explanation of what had happened.

Weeks after the house returned to normal, the family was still receiving requests from persons eager to "study" the house and interpret the "phenomena."

One physicist even charted "fields" that he believed were caused by water under the house. This, he said, was caused by a recharge basin, or sump, a mile away. The sump had been recently coated by thick ice. He thought that powerful vibrations caused by airplanes overhead might have jolted the ice so that shock waves were transmitted by underground water faults in such a fashion as to strike beneath the Herrmann house.

But the family no longer cared for any more investigations. James Herrmann said it didn't matter to him what moved the furniture and caused bottles to pop their tops in his home. And, as late as August 1958, the Duke parapsychologists were at a loss to explain the strange goings-on.

Mrs. Herrmann seemed to accept the events with amazing equanimity. She told Associated Press writer Joy Miller, "I don't think there is any definite solution. It was just one of those things with no rhyme or reason to it. But there was a definite physical force behind it."

Ordinary people. Extraordinary events. Pray they don't happen to you.

Legends of the Plains

The State Historical Society of North Dakota is housed in the modern North Dakota Heritage Center on the capitol grounds in Bismarck. Before the Society moved there in 1981, it occupied the Liberty Memorial Building, also on the Capitol grounds.

The Liberty Memorial Building is of 1920s vintage, designed to house several state offices, including the supreme court and the state library as well as the historical society. According to former employees, however, more than books and artifacts dwelt in the old building. They say a mysterious, ghostly presence, nicknamed the "Stack Monster," also stalked its hallways.

If appearances count for anything, the historical society's former quarters certainly fostered ghostly legends. Museum exhibits spilled over several floors, while hundreds of items acquired since the nineteenth century gathered dust in mazelike, subbasement rooms. Prehistoric skeletal remains, pioneer memorabilia, bound newspapers, and even some state records were stored in the cramped quarters. The entire place was eerie. The only light came from bare light bulbs hanging from cobwebbed beams.

A former superintendent of the historical society, James

Sperry, spent a considerable amount of time in the Liberty Memorial Building. Enough hours to wonder about two strange incidents he experienced during his years with the Society.

On a day in July 1972 Sperry was working late in his office on the second floor. It was about nine o'clock. A steady rain fell outside his windows. His collie/Lab mix dog, Shadow, snoozed at his feet.

Sperry got up to stretch his legs and wandered out of his office. He strolled down to the first floor where he found Frank Vyzralek, a society archivist, also working late. As they chatted, Shadow started to growl. Suddenly, she ran down the hall barking, then bounced down the steps leading to the basement storerooms. Within seconds she bolted back up the steps with her tail between her legs. Sperry and Vyzralek had no idea what Shadow saw or heard, or what scared her. They were quite sure they were alone in the building. But perhaps Shadow had seen or sensed something unsettling in the darkened basement.

On another occasion, Sperry alighted from the elevator in the basement. He saw a man in a white shirt walk back into a storage room. Though the light was dim, he thought it was a staff member and followed to find out who was down there. Sperry reached the room and turned on the light. He looked around. There was only the one doorway going into the room. It was impossible for anyone to have slipped past him. Yet the mysterious intruder had vanished.

Another witness to the Liberty Building's peculiarities was the archivist Frank Vyzralek. His experience that night with James Sperry was not the only time he worked late at night; he even came into the office on some holidays.

So it was that Vyzralek was in the old building late on New Year's Eve 1969. At about midnight, just before the turn of the new year, he was overwhelmed with the sensation that he should leave the building. "It was time to get out," he recalled thinking at the time. Though nothing untoward happened, he quickly shut off the lights and left.

Vyzralek's predecessor as archivist, Liess Vantine, swore he couldn't explain an incident in 1967. Vantine was working after regular hours with another employee, Craig Gannon. The other workers had left for the day. Leiss was in the subbasement when he heard a voice he thought was Craig's: "Come here, Liess."

Vantine wandered through the stacks and was surprised not to find his colleague nearby. Eventually, Vantine located Gannon several floors above, where he had been for over an hour. He had never called Vantine's name.

Walter Bailey, a historic preservation planner for the society, had an experience similar to Vyzralek's when he worked in the old building from 1973 until the move in 1981. On several occasions he would be overwhelmed with a sense that he should get out of the building. It was always at night and always when he was alone. Bailey described it as an urgent feeling, making him want to leave immediately, not ten minutes later. Nothing overt ever occurred; it was simply an understanding that he didn't belong in the building anymore—never any hostile force or a belief that he was actually in any physical danger. That he could see, anyway. And, Bailey said, the dread had nothing to do with the lateness of the hour (it usually transpired around midnight) or that he was usually alone. Bailey said he could be fully engrossed in a project when it happened. It was "like a bell going off in my head," he emphasized.

Bailey also heard occasional footfalls at night. Nothing similar occurred during the daytime because, as he recalled, the floors did not lend themselves to creaking or otherwise producing noises when they were walked upon by the crowd of daytime workers. When the footsteps were particularly distinctive at night, so that it seemed someone was in the building, Bailey always looked around for the interloper.

Without knowing it, Bailey may have produced a candidate for a nocturnal visitor. He said they seemed to come most often from the main floor, near the former society superintendent's office.

Russell Reid had been the Historical Society director for many years. As a bachelor, Reid devoted his personal and professional life to the Society. He often slept in his office. Could the spirit of such a committed civil servant have been responsible for the hauntings?

Or could it have been the former superintendent who startled Ron Warner late one night?

Warner, an administrative officer, returned to his office around eleven-forty-five after traveling out-of-town on Society business. As he entered the empty building, he heard someone cough. He stopped and listened and called out, "Who's there?" When no one answered, Warner looked around but all the office doors were locked and the lights turned off. He finally left, though he was always certain of what he had heard.

The so-called Stack Monster had not been heard from in the new Heritage Center. Maybe that's because Gloria Engel thinks the ghost left in the week before the move out of the old Liberty Memorial Building.

An administrative assistant, Engel was at her desk in the soon-to-be-vacated building. From her vantage point, she had a clear view of the large, heavy outside doors on the south side of the building. She was looking at the door when it very slowly opened, and then closed as if someone were going out. She saw no one near the door. Engel thought the Stack Monster left that day.

If the ghost, or whatever it is, decides to visit the new Heritage Center, it may encounter some difficulties. It will have to pass through a security system boasting the latest electronic equipment. All visitors and employees who enter the building must clear a security entrance and show special photo ID cards.

Fortunately, historians don't want to lose any part of the past, including historic monsters or ghosts. So, to make the move to the Heritage Center complete, the Stack Monster was reportedly issued its very own security badge. However, where the picture should be, there is only a gray background. Staff members want to make sure that the ghost feels welcome should it desire to check into some newer quarters.

The Writing Rock

On a high, windswept hill in the northwestern corner of North Dakota, a fieldstone shelter protects two gray granite boulders whose chiseled patterns have defied translation and interpretation. This is the Writing Rock Historic Site, established in 1936 by the State Historical Society to preserve these ancient and mysterious stones.

The larger rock, a ten-ton slab, is five feet high and four feet thick, and covered with hieroglyphs. Such pictographic writing is common to peoples throughout the world who do not have a written language.

The writing, filling the top and two sides of the rock, consists of lines, dots, circles containing dots, and the mythological figure of the thunderbird. The inscriptions are believed to have been carved at different periods, and many hypotheses have been put forth to explain their origin. At various times the pictographs have been ascribed to travelers from lost continents, wandering Norsemen, or Asian explorers. But anthropologists and historians think that the prevalence of the thunderbird may indicate that the markings were made by the Late Prehistoric Plains Indians.

Many years ago excavations of graves in the area yielded hammers and hatchets, seashells, arrowheads, elk teeth, and beads of various shapes and colors. In one grave beads were found that measured fifty-two feet when strung.

The Writing Rock site has always held supernatural significance for many of the Assiniboine, Sioux, and Plains Chippewa. Of the numerous Indian legends associated with the rock, the one heard most often was that told by Joe Lagweise and Tawiyaka, of the Qu'Appelle Agency in Saskatchewan, Canada. When these two Sioux were young men, in the 1870s, they visited Writing Rock and heard the story from an old man camped there.

In the days of the ancients, the old man said, eight warriors stopped for the night near the rock. Just as they were drifting into sleep they heard someone calling in the distance. Fearful of an enemy attack, they got up and searched, but found nothing wrong. They settled down again and the air was calm and the night peaceful.

In the morning they heard the voice again. It was clear and light, a woman's voice. No one could be seen. But, in their search, the Indians found the large rock. To their amazement, their own likenesses were pictured on the granite slab. All eight of them were shown with their packs spread on the ground. The warriors, unable to understand this phenomenon, continued on their way.

On their return they passed the rock again and saw that the picture had changed. It now appeared to show a scene from the future. The men hurried home and told their people. Then the entire village packed up and moved closer to the rock. Upon their arrival, the Indians saw that the picture had changed again—now it showed the village with its tipis.

From that time on the rock was believed to foretell the future. But that power was lost after white settlers moved the smaller rock to a spring about a mile from its original resting place. Later, this boulder was taken to the University of North Dakota for study. In 1956 the shelter over the large boulder was erected, and in 1965 the smaller rock was returned.

Crazy Loon

Buttes reach skyward, casting long shadows toward evening on the rolling plateaus near Amidon in southwestern North Dakota. South of that village, on the west side of U.S. Highway 85, is Black Butte, eight miles in circumference, with rock cliffs near the summit rising a hundred feet above the grassy slopes. At the base lie huge boulders, torn from the sides of the mesa by the action of wind, ice, and snow. Berries grow on the north side of the butte, while on the south side a cave holds the winter's snows until midsummer. From the top of the butte a splendid view unfolds for those sturdy enough for the climb.

During the latter years of the nineteenth century, Black Butte was called H.T. Butte because it was part of the H.T. Ranch, the largest horse ranch in the state. In those days the surrounding countryside was devoted to the ranging of cattle, sheep, and horses. It was only after the homesteaders arrived and began cultivating the land that ranching was curtailed.

At any rate, the H.T. Ranch required a large number of expert cowhands. Among those employed was a wrangler named Bob Pierce who, because of his merciless riding, was nicknamed "Crazy Loon." He rode his mounts everywhere at breathless speeds. It was hard for his boss to keep him in horses.

On one occasion, Pierce was teamed on the circuit with old Colonel Sullers. As the two set forth, the talkative colonel launched into a political discussion and pretended not to notice that his companion was spurring his horse to breakneck speeds. Sullers kept abreast, however, delivering what amounted to a monologue until his horse stepped into a hole and sent him flying.

Fortunately the old man's injuries were not serious. Cut and bruised, he limped to a nearby stream where he washed the dirt and blood from his head and face. Pierce turned back to join him.

The unhappy Colonel Sullers blamed Pierce for his injuries. "When you're dead," he said, shaking his finger at his younger companion, "your ghost will ride the top of the hills and howl like a gray wolf."

Bob Pierce subsequently died, killed perhaps on one of his wild rides. After his death a horseman was often seen on dark nights, galloping up the steep sides of Black Butte. Sometimes to the chilling howl of the gray wolf.

Holy Hills

Some three miles southwest of Cannon Ball, a small village south of Bismarck on the Missouri River, is a landmark known by the interesting name of Holy Hill. Just when or how the place was given its name is not known, but it was a place of spiritual significance to Native Americans.

A Sioux man named Joe Huff told one of the stories about Holy Hill:

In 1913, Huff was in Cannon Ball ready to return home when an elderly Sioux, Eagle Staff, asked Huff to go with him to his house for an overnight visit. Huff agreed and climbed in the wagon next to Eagle Staff for the journey to his log home.

Once arrived, they talked until late in the night. At last, Eagle Staff said, "Have you ever heard the spirits working on Holy Hill?"

"No," Huff replied.

"This is the month for the spirits to work," Eagle Staff explained, "but as they do not work every night I do not know if they will work tonight; if they do I will knock on your window and you can get up to hear them."

Huff went to bed and fell asleep. Soon, however, a knock at his window awakened him. Eagle Staff was there.

"Listen, the spirits are working," he said to Huff, who had dressed and gone outside.

Holy Hill was nearly a mile to the southwest, but Huff heard a clicking as if two rocks were being struck together. *Click, click, click, click.* And then a few seconds of silence until it would start up again.

Huff wanted to ride over to Holy Hill to investigate, but Eagle Staff said it would be useless.

"The spirits will leave as soon as you arrive. But if you have a good ear, get down on the ground and listen," Eagle Staff said.

Huff did as he was bidden. The clicks were even more clear when Huff placed his ear to the ground. It was like that for two miles around, Eagle Staff said. At ground level the clicks seemed to come from directly beneath, but when Huff stood again they drifted through the air from the direction of Holy Hill.

Eagle Staff had heard the mysterious noises since at least 1907. The clicks stopped in about 1923. Eagle Staff thought the spirits of Holy Hill were frightened away by the white people and their radios. What other explanation could there be?

The Deadly Wedding Gown

Could it be true that a North Dakota woman died because her sister's vengeful spirit returned on the woman's wedding day? Or, as the attending physician speculated, was embalming fluid the deadly agent? Either way, the story is extraordinary because it details a set of real events for an oft-told legend—a wedding gown that causes death for its owner.

There are two young women in this story, Lorna Mae Eberle and her sister, Carol. They lived in a small North Dakota town in the 1930s.

Lorna Mae was the younger of the two, with a cheerful disposition and extraordinary physical strength, a good prospect for one of the young farmers in the neighborhood. She was worth any two hired men, it was said, and certainly proved that on her family farm, which she ran virtually single-handed.

The older sister, Carol, was quite the opposite. Although prettier than Lorna Mae, she was sullen in her outlook on life and lazy around the house. The sisters shared the home with their father, an elderly farmer who usually gave in to Carol's petty demands. Mr. Eberle's wife, the girls' mother, had died in a tragic fire.

Carol Eberle may have lacked a pleasing personality, but she made up for that in being extremely strong-willed. What she demanded, she usually received.

But that did not extend to the man she most desired to marry.

His name was Ben Berg, a widower with three small children on a farm not far from the Eberles. Ben asked Lorna Mae to be his wife, as much for her ability to work side by side with him on the farm as anything else.

Carol was livid. She was far prettier than Lorna Mae, she told anyone who would listen, and so what if she wasn't a draft horse like her sister? Ben ought to be satisfied with marrying the loveliest girl in the entire county, she insisted.

Shortly before the wedding was to take place, however, Lorna Mae developed serious abdominal pains. Sister Carol was sent to fetch the doctor. Gossip had it that she dawdled in town before returning to the farm without the physician. She made vague comments about not being able to find the doctor. Lorna Mae was near death when Carol finally bundled her into a buckboard wagon and set off for the doctor's office. Lorna Mae Eberle died of a ruptured appendix soon after reaching town.

Carol saw the events as almost providential. She set about to make Ben Berg her husband, and to hell with common decency. At Lorna Mae's funeral, before the open casket bearing her dead sister in the wedding gown she had planned to marry in, Carol pleaded with Ben to marry her.

He was as aghast as the Eberle relatives who overheard the insensitive remarks. He put her off as best he could, saying it was far too early for him to think of a future without Lorna Mae.

The funeral services had ended and family and friends made their way out of the small church when Carol made her next move. She told the undertaker to remove Lorna Mae's wedding gown. Despite her father's outrage, she got her way.

"She won't have use for it in the earth," Carol sniffed. "A shroud will do as well."

And so it was that Lorna Mae Eberle went to her grave

wrapped not in her beloved wedding dress but in a simple pauper's shroud.

A month later Ben Berg gave in to Carol's persistent courting and agreed to marry her.

The wedding day was scheduled for a Sunday in mid-July. Guests sweltered in the one-hundred-degree heat, shifting uncomfortably in their wool suits. The soon-to-be Mrs. Carol Eberle Berg looked radiant in Lorna Mae's wedding dress. But suddenly she started to waver, clutching at her throat and gasping for air. She collapsed and died in Ben's arms, her tongue protruding from her mouth.

An autopsy failed to provide a cause for death. Heatstroke was ruled out, as was any other natural cause. What the doctor did offer as the reason for Carol's death, however, was hard for most of the townspeople to accept. He said that the high-necked wedding gown had absorbed some of the embalming fluid used for Lorna! The gown had been on Lorna Mae's body for three days before Carol removed it. Somehow, the doctor said, Carol's profuse sweating during the wedding ceremony had caused her pores to open too far and the deadly fluid to enter her body.

What most people believed, though, was that Lorna Mae's spirit had returned to strike down her evil sister. A ghost's revenge can be swift . . . and deadly.

Mr. and Mrs. G.

MURDER/SUICIDE
ORPHANS
FIVE CHILDREN

by
Bruce Trachtenberg
Oregonian Staff Writer

A Portland mother of five died of gunshot wounds early Sunday in an apparent murder/suicide in a north Portland home where she had sought refuge.

Her former husband turned the gun on himself after first shooting her, according to the Multnomah County Medical Examiner's Office.

Dead are Marles H., 36, and Billy H., 42.

Mrs. H. and the children had been living at the home of Mary L. Bellanger . . . where the shooting occurred.

"She came here in hopes of finding some protection," Mrs. Bellanger said. "We had known each other for about four and one-half years. We used to live next door to each other."

The Medical Examiner's Office said Mrs. H. was beaten and killed about 2:50 A.M. Sunday after she let her former husband in the house. (Billy) H. also died of a gunshot wound.

Arrangements for the five H——children await action by the Multnomah County Juvenile Court and the Portland Police Bureau of Youth Division.

Mrs. Bellanger said she hopes the children can spend Christmas with her family.

"I hope the Court is good enough to let the kids stay here for Christmas. We want to try to make this the best Christmas that we can make for them. We don't want to upset them anymore than possible."

The Police Youth Division said later Sunday the children would be allowed to spend Christmas at the Bellangers' home.

—Portland Oregonian, Dec. 24, 1973

The murdered woman didn't have a chance. She died just inside the front door, on a couch near a built-in cabinet with glass doors. The gunshots blew the glass doors to pieces. Blood was everywhere.

The five children and the Bellanger family escaped harm.

In 1973, *domestic violence* wasn't a term that most people had even heard of, let alone read about on the front page of their newspaper. Twenty years later it's impossible to determine what led a desperate man to murder his estranged wife two days before Christmas and then turn the gun on himself, to understand what horror raced through his frenzied mind that would move him to blow away a person he must have once loved.

But that unspeakable act reverberates still in the house where two lives ended.

The dead couple may haunt the Portland home in which their lives came to such a tragic end.

The three-story Victorian house looks much the same today as it did in 1973. It's in a north Portland neighborhood filled with turn-of-the-century homes built for managers and employees of a meat processing plant. They are well kept, although most are smaller than the one in which the couple died. Old sidewalks make an evening stroll inviting. Embedded in the curbs are the iron rings where suitors once tied their horses while calling on their sweethearts.

In the early 1980s, the house was put up for sale. Michael and Carolyn Brown were looking for a large, older home to buy and the place seemed perfect.

The Browns had first looked at the house when it was listed at $58,000, but didn't pursue the matter. When the price dropped even lower, the couple couldn't pass it up.

Carolyn Brown explained:

"Michael was with his mother and sister in Europe. Our other house was just a block away, so my mother and I decided to go through the house. I liked it. Michael and I had seen it before the original owner had moved out. When Michael called from Ireland I asked him to think about the house and when he came back we went through it again. We bought it."

The Browns offered $42,000, an amazingly low price considering the condition of the house and the generally high housing costs in the United States. Their offer was readily accepted.

The house was in good shape. The outside had been freshly painted, as had the interior. Beautiful fir floors had been well maintained.

New storm windows and carpeting to protect the floors were the only additions the Browns had to make. A previous owner had taken great pains to remodel the home. Even the heating system was in good shape.

Michael and Carolyn—with daughters Gennie and Cassie—moved in during November 1985. Their lives haven't been the same since.

Perhaps they should have paid closer attention to subtle indications that the house was . . . different.

"For a year and a half before we came, the house was vacant," Michael recalled. "Of course, the neighborhood kind of joked about the house being haunted, just because it was an old house, and it was vacant for [so long]."

The Browns didn't know anything about the murder/suicide twelve years earlier until the last owner stopped by while he was visiting the city.

"He came by to see the house," Carolyn said. "As he was leaving he just said, 'Oh, by the way, did you know there was a murder/suicide here?' We talked to the neighbors and they said there was a lady who had left her husband and came to this house with her kids. The husband came here real irate and killed her and . . . himself."

When she was a little girl, Carolyn imagined it might be exciting to live in a "haunted" house. She had no way of knowing her childhood fantasy might really come true.

"What was really strange," Michael added, "is that we both

had a strange feeling about the house. We didn't really discuss it between us, but we both felt that something was here."

The visiting former owner and neighbors confirmed their suspicions. "We both said bingo, that's it," Michael said. "There *was* something that happened here."

The first inkling that their "new" old house was *haunted* didn't occur until a year and a half after they moved in. At first, Carolyn thought her concerns came because of her self-described "active imagination."

"I just ignored it [feelings about the house]," she said. "I didn't mention anything to Michael, but I always had an idea, nothing specific, that there was something that we couldn't figure out about our home."

Six months later, Carolyn discovered that Michael, too, had the same wariness. She knew that it wasn't likely her husband imagined events. As a law enforcement officer for a Portland municipal agency, Michael is well trained as an objective fact-gatherer and observer. When the couple started comparing notes, however, they discovered a mutual inclination to believe that some things they attributed to chance or the natural creakings of an old house might be something more.

And when they found out about the murder/suicide, confirming the circumstances by reading the original news clipping, the Browns started wondering if there wasn't something to stories of murder victims haunting the houses in which they died.

A propensity to disbelieve the midnight frights of a small child eventually led to the first of nearly two-dozen separate encounters the Browns had with what they believe to be the ghosts of Marles and Billy.

"Cassie was the first one to see them," Carolyn said matter-of-factly. "She was nearly three years old. She would tell me that a lady was tucking her in bed at night."

"She said she was a very nice lady, and there would be a man off to the side. The man scared her. He would never smile, just watch. He never did anything mean, just watched. Something about him just scared her. The lady would pull the blankets up and tuck her in, and she'd go back to sleep," Carolyn recalled.

Because of her young age, Cassie had a hard time describing the night visitor. She knew, however, that the woman wasn't her mother. She said the woman had long hair. Carolyn's hair is short and usually permed.

Carolyn told Cassie it was a dream in order not to frighten the child, but she knew something else was going on.

"I have a bad habit of not tucking blankets under the mattress," she confessed. "I just pull them up so the kids can get out of bed if they need to."

When she checked on her daughter before going to bed, the blankets were usually tucked under the mattress and pulled tightly up to the child's chin. She assumed Michael had done it when he kissed his daughter good-bye before going off to his night shift. The mystery deepened during their later conversations—neither one had tucked the blankets under Cassie's mattress.

"Cassie wasn't afraid at all," Carolyn said. "She was just curious about why the lady was tucking her in. Of course, I kept telling her it was a dream." Carolyn knew her daughter wanted to believe that it was *only* a dream, yet at the same time saw that Cassie doubted her explanation.

The man lingering in the background was worrisome.

"He was a little behind the woman," Carolyn said of her daughter's description. "He wouldn't smile, just stand there. She didn't really want to concentrate on him because he made her nervous. 'I was a little scared of him,' she said. But the lady was nice."

The woman didn't make a sound except to whisper "shhhh!" as if quieting an unsettled child. Or stopping a little girl from crying out in fright at the sight of her ghost nanny.

Early in the fall of 1987, another incident involving the Brown children mystified Carolyn:

"Both girls were sleeping in Gennie's bed. Because we have a large house, heating can get expensive so we used an electric heater in the girls' room. Well, one night it was warm when we went to bed, but I woke up at about four-thirty in the morning, freezing. It was cold. I was worried about the kids so I went to their bedroom to turn on the electric heater. It was already plugged in and turned on. The room was warm."

The following morning, Carolyn asked her elder daughter if she had plugged it in.

"Oh no, Mom," Gennie answered. "I'm not allowed to do that."

"At least the kids were warm," Carolyn sighed, not wanting to linger too long on the unanswered question of just *who* plugged in the heater.

A second seemingly impossible event a few days later also dealt with appliances with minds of their own.

Some explanation is necessary. In the Browns' first-floor living room, one particular electrical outlet has a large adapter that will hold six separate plugs. In that adapter they have plugged in a television set, two VCRs, a lamp, and a cordless telephone. The latter has a particularly heavy plug-in, so large in fact that if it is accidentally knocked, the entire outlet adapter will fall out. If, for instance, Michael wants to unplug the lamp, he has to hold the wall adapter in place to do so.

Early one evening, Carolyn and the girls were out of the house and Michael was sleeping until his midnight shift started. Before he went to bed, he had set one of the VCRs to record a program from seven to eight o'clock.

Carolyn picked up the story:

"I got back home at nine P.M. Michael asked me why I unplugged the VCR. I told him I just got home. He said the VCR was unplugged, but his show was recorded. Nothing else was unplugged, just the one machine. It just couldn't have fallen out. No animals were in the house, in fact no one else was in the house and Michael was sleeping. There was no way that machine could have come unplugged at eight o'clock when no one else was home."

Michael, too, was stumped. "That was really tangible," he said. "That was when it was really confirmed [to me]. Prior to that, I thought there must be some logical explanation. But that VCR incident couldn't be explained because there was nothing that could have done that. I couldn't believe it."

Carolyn echoed her husband's sentiment. "We weren't sure how to react. There was a part of me that was a little excited that my childhood wish kind of came true, and yet I was nervous because of the kids."

The hauntings grew progressively more pronounced.

"There was one period when there was so much activity, footsteps and that sort of thing," Michael said, "that we wouldn't even go and look at one point. I remember us watching TV and we'd hear footsteps and not even bother to check."

Sometimes the incidents seemed prankish, such as the occasion during February 1988 when both the television set and radio came on by themselves.

"One night the kids spent the night over at Michael's mother's house," Carolyn remembered. "He was at work and I was upstairs sleeping. All of a sudden I heard this man's voice downstairs, booming. I grabbed Michael's gun and I went downstairs and the TV was on. Scared the wits out of me. I turned off the TV and I slept on the couch. I put Mike's gun under the couch. Then the radio upstairs turned on. I stayed on the couch."

Carolyn refused to go back upstairs. She said she wanted to be close to an outside door.

Within a few months, Carolyn seemed to arrive at an uneasy truce with the ghosts in her house, especially when they disturbed an otherwise peaceful night's sleep.

"During the summer—like that summer of 1988—when it's real hot, I let the kids sleep downstairs where it's cooler. Now one time I was sleeping on the couch, the kids were on the floor, and our husky/shepherd dog was sleeping with us. Sometime around one or two in the morning, I heard walking upstairs. From my bedroom to the girls' room, back and forth among the three bedrooms. My first reaction was that Cassie was looking for me. So I yelled up to her that I was downstairs. I still heard the walking. I got up and Cassie's sleeping on the floor with Gennie.

"The next logical thing was that Fairfax, our dog, was upstairs. I called to him and his head popped up next to me. At this point I was still hearing footsteps and I thought, well, Michael's at work and all of us are down here, so it must be Mr. and Mrs. G." Those were the nicknames she had given to the ghosts.

Carolyn wasn't about to let two ghosts keep her up all night.

"I went up to the landing and asked 'them' to stop walking around because they were going to wake up the kids."

"They" stopped.

When mysterious noises became too loud in the house, or the aimless walking disturbed her sleep, Carolyn again asked the ghosts to quiet down. Usually it worked, although she admitted feeling foolish for carrying on conversations with invisible people.

The ghosts were particularly noisy on another late night in 1988, Carolyn explained:

"I had just bought some furniture to go in Cassie's bedroom and there was no room for her to sleep in there, so Cassie slept with Gennie in her room. I heard knocking at maybe midnight or one o'clock in the morning. It sounded like it was at my door, but I wasn't sure. I said, 'Come in, Cassie!' But no one came in. The knocking stopped for a minute and then it came again, only louder.

"Fairfax, who was in my room, was scared. He wouldn't go to the hallway when I opened the door, thinking it was one of the kids who wanted me but wasn't coming in. There was nobody out there. I checked on the kids; they were both asleep."

At first, Carolyn thought her girls were playing a trick on their mother, a late-night game of "Let's scare Mommy!" She went back to bed, leaving her door slightly ajar so that she could see down the hallway. She expected to see one or both of the girls tiptoeing toward her bedroom. Instead, Carolyn found the phantom knocking had moved to another room.

"It was coming from Cassie's room," Carolyn said, which was unoccupied that night. "I wasn't sure, but it sounded like maybe the furniture or something in the wall. It kept getting louder the more I ignored it."

Once again, Carolyn got upset enough to scold the ghosts.

"It was like they wanted attention. So I said 'Okay, you got my attention, now knock it off! You're too loud, we're trying to get some sleep!!' The noise did stop. That seemed to work."

The Browns' large husky/shepherd dog, Fairfax, gave some clear indications to Carolyn that he, too, was wary of all the strange noises. "He'll do different things. He would always check on the kids in their bedrooms at night, always. He would hardly sleep, just go back and forth between their rooms. But when things were happening, like the knocking, he wouldn't leave me, in fact he would not even leave my bedroom."

When the family left the house for some reason, Fairfax went berserk. He chewed the blinds in the front room, and when they locked him in a pantry, gnawed on the doorframe trying to get

out. For a period of time they had Michael's sister look after him
in her home. He was fine there.

A new dog the Browns purchased, named Tuffy, seemed to
settle Fairfax a bit. Now the family puts both dogs in the backyard whenever they leave. But Fairfax intensely dislikes the third
floor and insists on sleeping in the master bedroom each night.
According to Carolyn, Tuffy doesn't exhibit any odd behavior in
any section of the house.

An air of protectiveness was also evident in the frequency and
intensity of the hauntings. Billy and Marles, if indeed they are
the ghosts as Carolyn and Michael Brown suspect, didn't take
kindly to visitors. On several occasions, the ghosts announced
their visits in most unsettling ways.

Carolyn's nephew, Jonah, got more than he bargained for
when he stayed over one night. "He heard arguing upstairs and
just assumed it was Mike and me," Carolyn remembered. "Well,
I was sleeping at the time and Mike hadn't even come home. Jonah didn't know that because he was sleeping on the couch. He
heard the arguing and tried to ignore it and then the voices
moved to the living room, around where the doorway is."

The doorway to which Carolyn was referring was the one that
once led to the kitchen from the entryway. It had been blocked
off some years ago. It was also the exact place where Billy murdered his wife and then turned the gun on himself.

Jonah had pulled the blankets up over his head, but decided to
peek after a few moments.

"He saw a woman and a man there arguing. They stopped and
looked at him and it scared the wits out of Jonah. He covered his
face and told her to go away."

After a few seconds of silence he looked again. They were
gone. For a very long time, Jonah would not visit his aunt and
uncle, and after that only if there was a large family gathering.

"He's feeling better, more secure," Carolyn said. "But that
was something that scared the poor guy."

A next-door neighbor, a woman named Nina, had two strange
experiences in the Browns' home. She often helped Carolyn
clean the three-story house. Once when she was on the third
floor working, while the Browns were gone, she heard a scream
come from somewhere in the house. Nina knew no one else was

with her. She quickly gathered her cleaning supplies and left for the day.

On another occasion, while dusting the second-floor landing, Nina heard the front door latch open. Someone walked across the floor downstairs. She called out that she was cleaning the staircase. She supposed Michael had come home early. Everyone else was gone. There was no answer to Nina's shout. Footsteps again crossed the first floor, the front door unlatched and then closed.

"She didn't work for us for very long," Carolyn said. "After that experience she said no thanks!"

Shortly after the Browns moved in, Carolyn's brother and his girlfriend came for a brief visit. They stayed on the third floor. A few nights after their arrival, the young woman was in the basement laundry room late washing clothes when a voice called out, "Hello down there!" She ran upstairs in the belief that someone had come into the house and was looking for a family member. No one was on the first floor. Carolyn and her daughters were asleep in the master bedroom.

"This was around the time that we did not believe things were happening," Carolyn said. The direct confrontations with their live-in ghosts were yet to come.

Carolyn was told about the incident the next day. "I just said it might have been the kids yelling down the laundry chute, but I was pretty sure that the kids were sleeping since they were in my bed. She didn't completely accept my answer and she didn't do the laundry after that."

The children—Gennie and her little sister Cassie—told their parents of numerous incidents in which they saw or heard the ghosts. One encounter even involved another well-known ghost story.

The girls had just seen a television adaptation of Oscar Wilde's "The Canterville Ghost." Cassie especially loved the story of Sir Simon's attempt to scare away an intrusive American family that inherits a haunted English castle.

Carolyn Brown picked up the story from there, on a night when Cassie wandered into her parents' bedroom:

"One morning around three o'clock, I heard Cassie calling, 'Sir Simon! Sir Simon! Please come back, I want to talk to you.'

I leaned over and told her to go to sleep, but I kept hearing her calling to him. It was in November 1989."

When her daughter wouldn't settle down, Carolyn realized something odd was going on.

"Who are you calling, honey?" Carolyn asked.

"Well, I saw Sir Simon, Mom," Cassie replied firmly.

"You saw Sir Simon what?"

"The ghost, Mom, the ghost!" Cassie declared.

Carolyn asked her to explain what she meant. She was half-asleep and not fully cognizant of what the little girl was trying to say.

"Well, Mom," Cassie started, "I came in here to climb into bed with you and he was standing there looking at you. Then he saw me and disappeared. But he didn't look like the guy on TV at all. He had kind of short hair like Dad and he wore clothes like Dad. He was kind of gray."

"Well, that's very interesting, Cassie," Carolyn said. "But why are you calling him to come back?"

"I want to invite him to my birthday party," Cassie replied, thinking that Sir Simon would be the perfect guest of honor at her upcoming birthday.

"Honey," Carolyn said carefully, "I don't think your friends would appreciate a ghost coming to your birthday party."

The Browns told their daughters early on that in all probability ghosts inhabited their house. "We had to be honest with them," Carolyn said. "How else could we explain all this stuff to them?"

Cassie talked about Sir Simon for days after. Her mother patiently told her that *their* ghosts were not the scary kind at all. They were good ghosts who plugged in heaters when the girls were cold or tucked them in bed. She explained the nice things they did. But to the girls, living in a haunted house was quite exciting. Gennie often told the stories to her friends at school.

Carolyn caution them about spreading too many tales.

"I told them not to tell their friends too much because they'd be too scared to come over. You have to be careful. And I've told them that some people don't believe in ghosts, so they know that."

Nevertheless, Carolyn laughed, "They think it's funny that their mom tells the ghosts to knock off the noise."

* * *

A month later, in December 1989 on the eve of Christmas, Gennie caught a glimpse of someone lingering around the Christmas tree. It wasn't Santa Clause.

"She had come downstairs and saw a man looking at the tree," Carolyn noted. Gennie apparently wanted an early glimpse of the presents she would be opening later that morning. "His back was to her. She got excited because she thought that maybe it was Santa Claus or her dad. Anyway, he turned around and disappeared."

At that, the child got scared and quickly returned to her bedroom. She didn't tell her parents about it until later.

What frightened Gennie was the sudden knowledge that the man next to the tree definitely wasn't her father and wasn't wearing a suit like Santa Claus. She later described him for her mother in ways similar to Cassie's description of her Sir Simon.

"I told her that it was Mr. G," Carolyn said. She said he was probably looking at the beautiful decorations the girls put on the tree and their fine presents.

Apparitions and disembodied voices became the norm for all the family members. Carolyn heard and saw unexplainable phenomena many times. "We'll see a white thing out of the corner of our eyes; it disappears when we turn around. Michael recently asked me if I ever saw a white apparition. I told him I thought I was the only one. I also hear a man's voice every once in a while. I'll be in the kitchen and I'll hear a man in the dining room. I'd think it was Mike and I'll come out and no one is there."

She said the words were indistinct, as if someone might be talking on the telephone or carrying on a hushed conversation.

At one point, Carolyn was in the living room when she heard a woman crying in the kitchen. At first she thought it might be Gennie or Cassie in some trouble. But when she called out for the girls, she discovered they were upstairs and had been there for quite some time.

The sudden, separate appearances of two ghosts frightened the Browns more than any other occurrence during their tenancy. Both times the ghosts decided to present themselves in the night.

"Mike was at work, the kids were sleeping, and I had my door cracked open," Carolyn said. "The hallway light is always left on. I woke up and I saw a man walking toward me. My first impression was that Mike had come home early, but then I realized he was still at work. We have a ceiling light that has a pull chain. I'm looking at him and scrambling for the light, swinging my arms back and forth looking for a chain. By the time I got the light on he had gone away.

"The light was coming in from the hallway so I couldn't see him too good, but it was more than a shadow. I could see his face a bit, not clearly, but I could see him. I slept with the light on after that."

The apparition's casual stroll toward her was so natural that Carolyn felt certain it was Michael. There was no anger or menace in his walk, only a slow deliberate pace that ended in the brilliance of the overhead light.

A dream vividly rendered? The power of suggestion arising from living in a haunted house? A trick of light? Carolyn doesn't think so. The man she saw was a solid, three-dimensional figure that looked for all the world like a human being. Only it wasn't.

Michael Brown's encounter with the ghost was so distressing that it stayed with him for days and weeks to come.

"I was on the early day shift so I had gone to bed earlier than the rest of the family," Michael recited. "I left the door slightly ajar and the hall light was on. I had just gone to sleep when some noise woke me up. I looked up and a lady was approaching me. I thought it was my wife in some kind of a gown or negligee. I seemed to lose track of time, except I could see she was more slender than my wife, her face was more slender and she had a different hairstyle. It was more of a straight hair style that went down to her shoulders. I actually thought it was my wife up until the time I put my arms up and the lady got really close. I realized it wasn't and that's when I let out a yell."

Carolyn came racing into the room. Her husband was sitting up in bed, the overhead light on. She asked him what had happened. He insisted everything was all right, he'd had a bad dream, that was all. He just wanted to go back to sleep. The next day, though, Michael told his wife that he'd almost embraced a ghost.

"That was the most tangible thing that's ever happened to me," Michael said. "That made a believer out of me."

* * *

Over the years Michael and Carolyn have grown accustomed to frequent reminders of their ghostly tenants. Not all of them are nearly as confrontational as the couple's nighttime visits from Billy and Marles.

Some incidents were merely annoying, while one seems to defy the laws of gravity:

- "Once Michael came downstairs," Carolyn said. "He'd been sleeping and the kids were in bed. He asked me if we'd been on the third floor. I said no. He told me there was someone walking up there. The kids were sleeping and the dog was downstairs with me. I told him he should go ask them to stop. He wouldn't. He said he would just stay downstairs with me for a while."

  Carolyn later performed her by now usual vocal exorcism. "When we went to bed, I asked them to please stop the noise, the walking around, because we were going to bed. It stopped."

- Strange things often happen on the house's third floor. The family uses it for storage and as a playroom for their daughters. It's well lighted, with a door that opens onto a sundeck. Sometimes it's too well lighted.

  Michael said: "I was across the street talking to a neighbor and I saw the lights on, which I thought was strange. I was walking back across the street to come home and the light went off."

  When he came in the door, Michael found his wife and children downstairs. No one had been on the third floor for some time.

  "The third-floor lights are always going on and off," Carolyn said. "I'd have to ask the kids if they'd forgotten to turn them off. It's really hard to tell when the kids forget to turn them off or when the lights are doing it by themselves."

  It happens often. The family leaves for a few hours in the evening, leaving the house in darkness, and when they return home lights are ablaze in various rooms. Gennie's bedroom lights are often popping on. With the exception of the bathrooms, all the ceiling lights on the second floor are operated by pulling on chains that hang down from them.

- A window in Gennie's bedroom has a peculiar habit of opening by itself. "During one period," Michael said, "I would find the window open, the inside window. The storm would still be closed. I'd shut the window and lock it and tell Gennie please not to open it. She said she wasn't doing it. I don't know how long it went on for, but it was almost a daily occurrence. I would shut the window again, and lock it, and then I'd find it open."

- Michael's paycheck stubs from work were the subject of one peculiar episode. "We keep them in a folder in the filing cabinet," Carolyn said. "I found them out by the kitchen telephone. Of course, Michael thought I took them out and I thought he had taken them out. They stayed there for about two months before he asked if I was done with them so he could put them away. I looked at him and said I didn't take them out. He said he hadn't. I asked the kids, too. Why would they be taken out? Why would they be there? They were just left in the kitchen. That was a strange thing." Perhaps ghosts, too, are interested in the financial affairs of the living.

Despite the puzzling episodes with lights, windows, relatives, knockings, footsteps, and even mysterious figures in the night, none seemed particularly violent. If the Browns didn't precisely "accept" the presence of ghosts in their fine old Victorian home, neither were they especially frightened by anything that happened. It never entered their minds to give up the house.

The closest Carolyn Brown came to feeling that the ghost couple could cause some harm came on Christmas Eve 1990. It involved, of all things, mixed nuts.

The Browns had the family Christmas celebration at their house as usual because it could accommodate everyone. Carolyn's sister-in-law had brought a plastic tray filled with a variety of fresh nuts. All of their relatives had left and Carolyn was cleaning up in the kitchen. Michael had gone to bed. The children were sleeping.

"I was putting some stuff away and noticed that the tray with the nuts was halfway off the table," Carolyn recalled. "I pushed it back on the table and then I started putting things away again. And then the tray just flipped backward. It was like someone had taken his hand underneath and flipped it up. The tray hit the wall and nuts scattered everywhere."

Carolyn turned off the lights and ran upstairs.

She didn't tell her husband why she suddenly appeared in the bedroom. The next morning, Michael discovered the mess in the kitchen and cleaned it up. He asked her what happened. "I asked him if he remembered me coming upstairs so suddenly? I told him what had happened. I didn't feel like cleaning up the nuts at that point."

In early August 1992, a new twist was added to the Brown family haunting.

Carolyn was making plans to paint the ceilings in several rooms. She had carefully surveyed the ceilings to determine how much paint would be required. But one morning her plans were put on hold. As she looked over the living room ceiling, she noticed four brown-colored streaks extending only a few inches in one area.

"It looked like someone had taken his thumb and three fingers, rubbed them in dirt and then dragged them across the ceiling," Carolyn said. The marks were not there the day before, she emphasizes, because she had examined the section of the ceiling.

The high ceilings cannot be reached even with the tallest stepstool in the house. No workmen had been in the house. There seemed to be no logical explanation for how they got up there. The mysterious smudges remained there for months afterward.

To add to this new mystery, only a few days before the discovery of the ceiling marks, one of the ghosts made an audible appearance.

Michael was working the overnight shift and therefore Carolyn wasn't surprised when she heard the bedroom door open shortly after daybreak. Dozing lightly she heard her husband walk toward her. But the footfalls quickly retreated from the room, and down the hallway. The next thing she knew the front door opened and slammed shut, causing a wind chime hanging on the door knob to tinkle.

A bit upset by what she considered her husband's bizarre behavior, Carolyn came downstairs to investigate. Michael was coming in the back door. He had been taking out the garbage and had not been anywhere near their bedroom. He, too, had heard the front door slam shut and wondered who was up at such an early hour. The couple looked at each other and knew immediately that it was another piece added to their ghostly puzzle.

Michael and Carolyn Brown haven't seriously considered moving from their home, especially since the entities never seem to upset the children or want to harm them. If there had been the slightest indication that the entities were evil or malicious, Carolyn said they would have moved away. Their experience has been characterized more by a peaceful coexistence. The ghosts don't seem to dislike the Browns, they just want to impress upon them their indelible presence.

"We've basically accepted them," Carolyn said. "We do get scared and would like it if they go. But the kids were concerned that the ghosts might me going away. They don't want them to. The kids want them to stay. It's exciting to them.

As to why their house is haunted, Carolyn has had a lot of time to think about that:

"He [Billy] made a mistake. Is he sorry for what he did? Is he trying to make amends? I try to come up with my own interpretation. And I feel honestly that the lady likes being close to the kids, tucking them in. She misses her kids and wants to look after ours. Nothing negative has ever happened really, I mean besides getting scared once in a while. But nothing truly threatening."

Michael and Carolyn think that the murder/suicide was an act of passion involving only the former occupants. Their ghosts don't harbor any ill will toward the living.

"I feel relieved that nothing negative has happened. We can make this whole ghostly situation a positive thing as much as possible. We can't afford to move and we don't really want to move yet. I really like the house. There's a lot we can do, especially when the kids reach their teens," Carolyn noted.

The couple have plans for remodeling the third floor into a master bedroom with a sitting room and art studio. The girls would have the second floor, while the couple's present bedroom would become the family room.

In the meantime, Michael plans to research the history of the house and find out as much as he can about the circumstances surrounding the deaths of Billy and Marles. He wants to know the personalities of the couple who linger long after death in the house where they died.

"The ghosts are pretty respectful of us," Carolyn summarized. "I think part of it is that we try not to react too much. I just tell them to stop what they're doing. Of course, they do give us a start now and then."

When necessary, however, Carolyn is stern with their supernatural guests. "I told them not to show themselves in front of the kids. I will not have them scaring my children!"

Even the most pertinacious phantom is no match for a mother protecting her children.

NOTE: Certain names in this story were altered to protect the privacy of some individuals, living and dead.

Ghosts of the Grand Strand

Sixty miles of wide, white beaches, known as the Grand Strand, frame the Atlantic Ocean off the coast of South Carolina. Warmed by the Gulf Stream, the area has become a popular tourist mecca visited by fishermen, golfers, sunseekers, and those who wish to do nothing more than enjoy the beauty of this land.

Here, a visitor might see, beyond a grove of magnolias, the ruins of a nineteenth-century rice plantation, or glimpse a figure sweeping through a shadowed alley of live oak trees hung with moss. Was the figure real? Maybe. Maybe not. The ghostly legends of the Low Country are numerous. They've been handed down through many generations, and the natives are usually pleased to share them.

Here are two of the most popular stories:

The Warning

Pawleys Island is a sliver of beach joined to the South Carolina mainland by two short causeways. It's an unpretentious kind of place with no high-rise hotels, no condominiums, no golf courses or fast-food restaurants. No neon, either. Southern gentry live simply in weatherbeaten cypress cottages built by their ancestors. In the summer they enjoy trapping crabs in the tidal creek separating the island from the mainland, lazing in a hammock, or strolling the sands while watching the gulls wheel overhead and the surf roll in.

That's what island residents Jack and Clara Moore were doing on the evening of September 19, 1989—walking the beach and enjoying the beauty of the fading day. Suddenly, a man appeared and walked past them. As they turned to speak to him, he seemed to vanish. The couple didn't think there was time for him to duck into a house or behind a breakwater.

Who had they seen? Clara Moore thinks it could have been the Gray Man of Pawleys Island, the legendary specter who appears before each hurricane to warn residents to leave. Though the man they saw didn't say anything, the Moores didn't need a warning. They were already packed.

At midnight on Thursday, September 21, 1989, Hurricane Hugo boiled up out of the east and crossed the South Carolina coast. The screaming 135-mile-per-hour winds spun buildings, boats, and trees through the air, cutting electrical power and plunging the barrier islands into terrifying darkness. The eye of the storm, arriving at high tide as it did, hauled a tower of water seventeen feet above ocean level. Pawleys Island was devastated. Fourteen houses were destroyed and dozens more were damaged. Some were blown across to the mainland. An inlet was cut at the southern end of the island and into the inlet a house was dropped, its pink shutters still intact. Not since Hurricane Hazel, in 1954, had a storm wiped out the South Carolina coastline.

Automobile dealer Bill Collins would never forget Hazel. He and his bride were honeymooning in a Pawleys Island cottage in October of that year. Early one morning someone knocked at the door. Collins thought he was dreaming and rolled over to go back to sleep. He couldn't. The knocking persisted. Cracking one eye open, Collins noted the time on his bedside clock—5:00 A.M. Who comes calling at that hour? No one except a neighbor in distress. Yet the island was almost deserted on that October day in 1954.

Collins crawled out of bed and padded barefoot to the door.

On the porch stood an old man in rumpled gray pants, gray shirt, and a gray cap pulled so low on his forehead that the features of his face were shadowed. Collins had never seen him before.

"The Red Cross sent me to warn everyone to get off the island," the stranger began. "Big storm blowing in."

Collins smelled the brine on the man's clothes. Suddenly he was gone.

"He just vanished," Collins told his bride, who was now awake. Only the urgency in the old man's voice persuaded the couple to get out. Within an hour they were back on the mainland, in nearby Georgetown, and a short time later Hurricane Hazel hit Pawleys Island. It was one of the most devastating storms of this century.

When the Collinses returned to the island, they found that most of the cottages had washed out to sea and dunes thirty feet high had disappeared. Yet their house was untouched by the storm's wrath. Towels that Mrs. Collins had hung on the porch to dry were still there, as was the TV antenna on the roof.

Collins had met the ghost of the Gray Man—that benevolent specter who looks out for the residents of the island. Legend says that no harm will come to those who see him.

The Gray Man first materialized before the storm of 1822. Even though the rice planters who settled the island knew they'd built in the path of hurricanes roaring up the coast from the Caribbean, the likelihood of savage storms striking the island seemed remote.

The daughter of one planter was spending a summer on the island, awaiting the arrival of her fianceé, who had been abroad for several years. He returned safely to Pawleys, but, in taking a shortcut through a bog, his horse stumbled and fell. Quicksand devoured man and beast.

The grief-stricken girl walked the beach day and night. One windy day she saw a man in gray coming toward her. Recognizing her dead lover, she ran to him with arms outstretched. But before she reached him he was swept into the sea. Her father, upon learning of the incident, was convinced his daughter was suffering a mental breakdown and rushed her to a Charleston hospital. She was pronounced in excellent health.

The next day a hurricane hit the island and raged for two days. Stunned survivors mourned the dead, then cleaned up the litter and rebuilt their homes. In time the island of oleander and oak trees became again an oasis of peace and beauty.

So the island remained for seventy-one years. And during all that time the story of the mysterious man on the beach was told and retold. A legend had been born. The Gray Man, it is said, would always come to warn the islanders of an approaching storm.

One day in 1893, an odd-looking man appeared at the door of a French family named Lachicotte. The visitor was dressed in gray from head to foot. He said nothing, but shuffled his feet, then turned away. The Lachicottes fled their home immediately. Others were less fortunate.

The day that had begun as sunny and pleasant, with a breeze stirring the curtains at open windows, turned sullen. The sky darkened while at the same time the sea appeared to be on fire. The tide never ran out; it came thundering up over the sands until the entire beach had vanished. Trees snapped, their limbs exploding like firecrackers. Birds beat their wings helplessly, seeking sanctuary from the roar of winds and water.

Whole families died, perhaps none more pathetically than members of the Flagg family, who were vacationing at their summer homes on Magnolia Beach, now Huntington Beach State Park north of Pawleys Island.

When the sea washed under the doors of the cottages, young Dr. J. Ward Flagg and his parents climbed as high as they could into a beach cedar tree. The surf churned over them. Old Mrs. Flagg was the first to go, on a wave forty feet high. Her husband, seeing her vanish, let go his grip and went after her.

When the storm abated, the sea turned back and the sun came out. Rescuers reaching young Dr. Flagg, or "Wardie," as they called him, had to pry loose every one of his fingers from a bough of the tree. A small niece and a servant escaped death with him, but the doctor's brother, the brother's wife, and five children all lost their lives.

A baby's shoe and undergarment swung from a barren treetop; a woman's shoe, unbuttoned to the last button, stuck up in the sand like a hideous marker; clothing, splintered furniture, and shards of glass that had once been cottage windows littered the beach.

Day and night survivors searched for bodies. A wagon loaded

with empty coffins rumbled across the strand, and whenever a body was found it was placed in a coffin and taken to the porch of a neighboring church. Ministers were kept busy praying for the dying and conducting funerals for the dead.

The water, rising a foot higher than Hazel, was the result of what is said to be the worst storm in South Carolina history.

Dr. Flagg never fully recovered from the tragedy. He locked himself inside the house on land that is now part of Brookgreen Gardens, and the seasons passed without his knowledge. With window shades lowered, he saw neither sunshine nor rain. Friends tried to encourage him to leave the cottage, but he refused. Dr. Flagg's loyal servant, Tom Duncan, who survived the storm with him, kept house for him.

Finally, the doctor did leave his house. There was no one else to tend to the sick of the area. He also served as postmaster, but whenever he could he paced the beach, gazing out to sea and stooping to pick up articles washed in on the tide. He told Tom that as he walked the sands his mother, father, and the rest of his relatives spoke to him. Their voices brought him solace.

It is said that even today those persons keen of eye and ear may see the misty forms of the Flaggs and hear their pitiful cries.

And, although the Coast Guard now alerts residents of incoming storms, the Gray Man of Pawleys Island still makes his rounds, shuffling from cottage to cottage to deliver his warning. Is he the lover who was killed? Or just a nameless shipwrecked sailor? Does it really matter?

NOTE: Dr. J. Ward Flagg was a nephew of Alice and Allard Flagg (see following story).

The Lovely Lady of Hermitage

ALICE. A single name on a flat marble tombstone. A child of sixteen dead of typhoid fever. And today, nearly 150 years after her death, her ghost walks, searching for a ring.

The story begins in 1848 when Alice Belin Flagg, her brother, Dr. Allard Flagg, and their widowed mother moved into the Hermitage at Murrells Inlet. Alice loved the plantation house with its imposing white pillars, wide brick steps, and large rooms, which were light and airy. The building, of imperishable pitch pine, had taken slaves four years to build.

But Alice's happiness would be short-lived. She fell in love with a turpentine dealer.

The news devastated Mrs. Flagg. Ever conscious of the family's place in South Carolina aristocracy, she warned her daughter, "Child, he is beneath our station. He will disgrace our family name and bring you nothing but unhappiness." Her voice was hard and sharp.

Alice turned to her brother. "You heard her," said Dr. Allard, as everyone called him. "He's nothing but a common laborer." He lit his pipe and stared at his sister above the flame of the match. The muscles of his face tightened. "Mother and I forbid you to see him."

But Alice did see him—many times, in a grove of oak trees far from the house. It became their secret trysting place.

One afternoon Alice told her lover to come to the house the next day. She'd be home alone. Her mother would be in Charleston and her brother would be attending several critically ill patients. He came—a tall, slim man with erect bearing and a kindly, reassuring face. From his pocket he brought forth a tiny box, took out the diamond ring and slipped it on her finger. The gem caught the light, reflecting it in long silver rays. Alice and her lover embraced. At that moment Dr. Allard walked into the room. "Get out!" he roared.

Alice watched her lover stride from the room, but made no attempt to follow him. Her brother drew near and stood silently before his sister. Then he pulled the ring from her finger. "Alice," he said in a voice now calm and composed, "you will break your mother's heart and mine too if you marry that man." He paused and turned the ring in his fingers. "But he has given you this ring. It is not mine to dispose of. If you'll wear it on a ribbon concealed in the neck of your dress, mother will never know."

Alice nodded and fought back the tears.

Early one morning two weeks later, Mrs. Flagg discovered the ring on the chest in her daughter's bedroom. She shook Alice awake and demanded an explanation. When none was forthcoming she screamed invectives at both Alice and the absent lover. Alice pulled the bedclothes high up under her chin. She felt sick.

Then the door banged open and Dr. Allard entered the room. He noticed the ring on the chest. "Mother, you've had a restless night," he began. "Come along now and let me give you a sedative." She went willingly, supported by her son's strong arms. As their footsteps receded down the hallway, Alice knew that she could no longer remain in the house. She would be sent away to a boarding school in Charleston. Her mother and her brother had discussed that possibility at one time. Alice buried her face in her pillow and wept.

Dr. Allard drove his sister to Charleston, the carriage jouncing over broken sections of roadway and the steamer trunk rattling in the rear. The trip, a distance of about eighty miles, took four days.

At first Alice was excited by the sights and sounds of the city. King Street and Meeting Street were filled with the bustle and banter of shoppers and the clatter of horses' hooves on the paving. Shade trees of every variety lined the streets, and after dark the gaslights shone softly on the leaves.

But the novelty of these distractions soon paled. Alice could not concentrate on her schoolwork. Although she tried to complete the daily assignments, her heart was elsewhere. She overslept her classes. Her new friends, noting her listlessness, tried to help her. Unsuccessfully.

But by the time spring came Alice's spirits soared. The school term would soon end and she could return home to her beloved. At the May Ball, Alice, resplendent in a white gown, glided across the floor with one young man after another from Charleston's aristocracy. Her eyes shone brilliantly and a high color came into her cheeks. But she would not remember this night.

Early the next morning Dr. Flagg was notified to come and take his sister home. She had become critically ill.

Allard Flagg set out immediately. At the school he wrapped his sister in blankets and placed her in the carriage. A friend had packed the gown.

Upon reaching the Hermitage, Alice was put to bed immediately. Typhoid fever had struck, as it did every spring in the Low Country. The physician could only try to keep his sister as comfortable as possible during her remaining hours.

Alice soon realized that her ring was not on her finger and

cried out for it. Legend has it that her brother had thrown it into a creek on the way home. A sympathetic cousin soon appeared with a ring, but Alice, even in her delirium, knew it wasn't hers and threw it on the floor. Two days later she lapsed into a coma and died.

Alice's mother was not with her dying daughter. Like many other residents of the swampy coastal area, she spent the months of May through September in the mountains to escape the deadly fevers so prevalent during the warm weather. Unwilling to call his mother home, Dr. Allard had his sister dressed in her ball gown and the coffin lowered into a temporary grave on the plantation. Later, in the presence of the grief-stricken family, the body was permanently buried in the Flagg family plot in All Saints Waccamaw Episcopal cemetery, three miles west of Pawleys Island.

But Alice does not rest easily. When the moon is full and a mist rises over the fields of the Low Country, she returns to the home she loved. Some say she still searches for her lost engagement ring. So many have reported seeing Alice that she may be the most authenticated ghost of the Grand Strand. She always appears in her beautiful ball gown.

Since 1910 the Willcox family has owned the antebellum home. Clarke Willcox and his wife, Lillian, both now deceased, never saw Alice, but one member of the family saw the lovely apparition many years ago.

During Clarke Willcox's childhood his mother's sister, "Aunt Lolly," often visited her only sister's family. Early one morning Aunt Lolly was seated at the vanity brushing her hair. Suddenly, in the mirror, she saw the bedroom door open and a young girl enter the room. When the girl did not speak Aunt Lolly swung around. No one was there. Hairbrush in hand and screaming, the woman flew down the stairs. She never slept in that room again.

Through the years a number of superstitions have arisen about Alice. Young people say that if you walk thirteen times backward around the grave you can commune with her spirit. It's said that once a young woman walking in the opposite direction saw her own ring fly off her finger. Friends spent most of the day trying to find it.

Red roses or camellias often appear on Alice's tombstone. No one knows who brings the flowers, but some believe that the ghost of her lover has something to do with it.

NOTE: The water surge from Hurricane Hugo in 1989 reached the front porch of the Hermitage, but did not enter the house, which suffered relatively minor damage from fallen trees.

Clara and Lizzie

Thirteen-year-old Clara Robertson was alone practicing the piano when it happened. Someone walked down the long hallway of the boarding school and entered the music room where she sat engrossed in her lesson. It would be a classmate, she thought. It wasn't. Clara looked up into the skeletal face of a little girl. The specter wore a tattered pink dress streaked with green mold; tangled locks of black hair hung to her shoulders. Rotted teeth protruded from a fleshless mouth.

Clara screamed, fled into a nearby bedroom and leaped into bed with another girl who was stricken with the flu. The ghost followed and, gliding silently to their bedside, began to tug at Clara's hair. Unable to speak, Clara buried her face in a pillow and waved her arms to chase the hideous thing away. Moments later, the two frightened children rushed downstairs to report what had happened.

Fellow students snickered. There was no such thing as a ghost, they said. Not in the prestigious albeit curiously named Brinkley Female College, an academy for small girls. Not in Memphis, Tennessee. Certainly not in 1871.

Of course, tales of a haunting *had* surfaced from time to time at the boarding school, but they revolved around the founder, old Mr. Brinkley. He'd gone bankrupt, then insane. A few people thought that his restless spirit roamed the rooms of the gloomy antebellum mansion on DeSoto Street (now South Fifth Street). But a ghost child in a pink dress? Never.

Only Clara had seen the supposed ghost. Her sick chum couldn't verify any of the report. Humiliated and fearful, Clara did not sleep that night. The next afternoon she practiced the piano. No ghost appeared.

But on the third day the specter was back. Two students were with Clara in the music room when they were bewildered by a strange sound, as if someone were splashing water onto the floor. In the next moment, all three girls saw the hideous, grinning girl in the mildewed clothing. The pungent smell of damp earth filled the room.

The girls ran shrieking down the staircase and, in their haste, bumped into a startled Jackie Boone, a young instructor. She calmed them down, then agreed to return to the music room with them.

The little spirit was still there. Or so the girls said. The teacher saw only an indistinct shadow in the far corner of the room. She told Clara to ask the ghost what it wanted.

"Do not fear me," the girl ghost told Clara. "My name is Lizzie. I was the last to die in my family. Treasure lies buried five feet deep under the old stump behind this house. Please dig it up, Clara. I want you to have it." With those words the ghost faded away.

Miss Boone said she hadn't heard any of the speech, only an odd rumbling noise.

Within the week the story got out. Memphis newspaper headlines screamed the salient facts:

BRINKLEY FEMALE COLLEGE HAUNTED AND IN AN UPROAR OF TERROR AND CONFUSION.

THE GHOST MAKES A 'KENO'

FURTHER SUPERNATURAL AND STARTLING REVELATIONS FROM BRINKLEY COLLEGE

Fear gripped the city. Frightened mothers kept lanterns burning through the night, children cried if left alone, and men who had to be out at night fortified themselves with a "Ghost Cocktail" concocted by some enterprising Memphis bartender.

Dr. Meredith, principal of the school, ordered a thorough investigation. *Pranksters*, he grumbled to himself.

Meanwhile, Clara's father, J. R. Robertson, a Memphis attorney and civic leader, hired a spiritualist medium named Mrs. Nourse. The medium gave Clara pencil and paper and explained that messages from the spirit world would be given to her and she must write them down exactly as they were given. It would be Clara's first experience with automatic writing.

The medium put Clara into a trance. After she had lapsed into glassy-eyed slumber, neighbors who'd been invited to the séance asked their questions.

Who *was* the ghost, they wanted to know. In an unfamiliar hand, Clara wrote, "Lizzie Davidson." Old-timers recalled that the mansion had been built before the Civil War by a Colonel Davidson, and that the family's eight-year-old daughter, Lizzie, had died there in 1861. They remembered that the child had been buried in a pink dress rather than the customary white.

Other spectral messages arrived unbidden: The Brinkley family had no legal claim to the property, one claimed. Davidson's deed to the land was inside a large glass jar, along with coins and jewelry. The jar, buried beneath a stump, must be found by Clara Robertson herself. Or so the messages asserted.

Mr. Robertson became uneasy during the séance. He wanted to believe his daughter's stories about the little ghost girl, but his keen analytical mind couldn't accept this venture into a world far removed from reason. At the same time, he was fascinated by the writing penned by Clara, writing that she would never recall composing. After much deliberation, Mr. Robertson decided to schedule more séances in his house. After they yielded corroborative evidence, he thought it was his duty to help Clara locate the jar. He discussed his plans with Dr. Meredith. The principal agreed the "treasure" should be found.

Beneath a pale moon on a frosty February night, several men with shovels dug deep trenches around the old stump. The sound of picks striking rocks sang in the night air. After several hours of fruitless digging, the workmen were dismissed until daybreak. A few broken bricks were their only discoveries.

When the pick-and-shovel gang returned at dawn, Clara and her father were among the first arrivals to watch the work. The stump was finally pulled frees, and as Clara gazed down into the deep hole, the spirit appeared to her. No one else saw it. The ghost chided her for not seeing the treasure herself. Clara slithered down into the hole, lifted a heavy pick, but couldn't swing it. She fainted. Her father then took over the job. Ten minutes later, he'd unearthed a five-gallon Mason jar! It was tightly sealed, and although partially covered with mold, bags and packets could be seen inside. Also a large yellow envelope. The missing deed? Then, in the strangest of all of the episodes, Clara said the spirit's voice warned that since Clara herself hadn't uncovered the jar, it must not be opened for sixty days.

Mr. Robertson took the jar home with him, but soon had to summon the police to protect his house from mobs of people, all demanding to see the mysterious container.

Then he announced his new plan. Clara and her father would open the jar on the stage of the old Greenlaw Opera house, at the southwest corner of Union and Second, on the morning precisely sixty days from the moment their find had been unearthed. Admission would be one dollar, half of the money to be given to Clara in partial compensation for the "terror and suffering" she had endured, and the other half to benefit the city's orphans.

But, one night just before "Opening Day," J. R. Robertson heard a noise in his backyard and went to investigate. When he did not return promptly, servants went looking for him. They found the attorney lying unconscious in a pool of his own blood. His head had been slashed and red marks on his throat seemed to indicate that he'd been choked.

He was able to tell this story: As he'd stepped out the back door, three men jumped him. One pistol-whipped him about the face, another seized him around the throat. A third attempted to scalp him with a long knife. They demanded that he turn over the jar. Robertson told them it was suspended by a rope *beneath the seat in the outhouse*! Repugnant though the hiding place was, the ruffians found the jar and fled with it.

Though it was never seen again, the jar's contents were allegedly revealed to Clara in another séance. A newspaper account said that the jar contained two thousand dollars in gold, a diamond necklace, gold jewelry, and some "important papers."

Was Clara a serious young spiritualist or only a bored adolescent bent upon creating a little excitement? Did her father stage the "jar robbery" to avoid splitting the find with others? No one knows. But her story has passed into legend and is still considered Memphis's most fascinating ghost story.

At the end of her schooling, Clara Robertson married a fellow spiritualist and, although she conducted many séances, the sad little ghost in the torn pink dress never appeared again.

Brinkley Female College itself faced a series of financial crises and eventually closed. The building then became a tenement for railroad workers. As surrounding houses were razed, the great gray mansion stood alone, its paint peeling, its massive front pillars crumbling—a fading specter itself of another time.

In 1972 the house was demolished. The ghost girl was gone forever.

The Three Nephites

To appreciate the stories of the Three Nephites, it is necessary to know that the doctrine of the Church of Jesus Christ of Latter-day Saints (the Mormons) holds that after Jesus' ascension from the Holy Sepulchre, he appeared in South America to persons known as the Nephites. Jesus taught them that they had been chosen by God to know the true gospel and to teach it to the nonbelievers. This was the beginning of His ministry in the New World.

Then, as proof of His Godhead, Jesus raised a man from the dead and performed other miracles similar to those he had performed earlier in Judea. Before His ascension into Heaven, Jesus appointed twelve new apostles from among the Nephites and asked them what they desired. Nine asked to be raised up when their earthly work was finished, and three asked to remain on earth forever, doing His work.

And so it was that when the Mormons first settled the land that would become the state of Utah, these three wandering patriarchs appeared, bringing hope and courage to those early pioneers who struggled to clear the land, to fight the great plagues of locusts and grasshoppers, and to survive the periodic droughts in the harsh environment of the great American West.

For 150 years these holy men, the devout believe, have roamed the towns, villages, and isolated settlements of this intermountain state; there is scarcely a locale that has not been touched in some way by the Three Nephites with their bone-white feet, their long, flowing white hair and beards.

They travel singly by most accounts, arriving unseen, unbidden, often seeking a meal or simply a place to stay the night. They come on foot, usually, less often by a rickety cart pulled by an ancient nag. They cure the sick, bring prosperity to the poor. The host who shelters a Nephite never learns his true identity until after he has left. After the stranger vanishes, leaving no earthly trace whatsoever, the Mormon family believes they have been touched by the hand of God.

The Nephites remain on earth voluntarily. Although the earliest reports of their encounters with faithful Mormons came from Utah, later stories started coming in from all over the world as the Nephites supposedly followed Mormon missionaries who sought converts in every part of the globe.

Eminent folklorists such as E. F. Fife, Richard M. Dorson, Hector Lee, and Jan Harold Brunvand have spent years collecting stories of the Three Nephites, and their files contain hundreds, if not thousands, of sightings. The Three Nephites evidently appear to persons in all strata of society, and have for the past century and a half. They have not gone away, even with more sophisticated methods of transportation and a generally skeptical population. Encounters are reported even today.

Whether rooted in theology or folklore, fact or fiction, or somewhere in between, individual experiences are worth the telling.

One spring day in 1852 an old man knocked at the door of a family living in Salt Lake City and asked if he might eat with them. The Mormons had settled the area only five years earlier, and hardships were evident everywhere. The woman of the house hesitated only momentarily, then invited the wayfarer to share the family's humble meal of water, bread, and onions.

He ate quickly, then asked what he owed her. When she refused his money, he left, saying, "May God bless you. Peace be with you."

The woman ran to the door, but the man was gone. When she turned to clear the table she noticed that his food was still there, uneaten!

During years of drought when this woman's neighbors were starving, her larder was always full. She *knew* it had something to do with the stranger's visit.

One summer evening, two young women on horseback were trapped on a mountainside when their horses panicked before a crevice filled with sliding shale. The animals refused to move forward or backward. One of the women, a devout Mormon, dismounted and scrambled to the mountaintop, hoping to find a hiker or perhaps a prospector. But the area was deserted. Picking up a willow switch, she returned to her companion. They took turns flailing the horses, but nothing could get them to move.

Suddenly, a voice called out from somewhere above them. "Sister, how did you come here?"

Incredibly the women found themselves and their horses in the next instant on top of the mountain. They had no recollection of how they got there. A bearded man in clean blue overalls helped them ride safely away from the dangerous cliff edge.

The young Mormon rider turned to thank their benefactor, but of course he was not in sight.

She nodded to her friend. "That was one of the Nephites."

Niels Nielson was finishing up chores when the wagoner drew up to the barn. "I was wondering if you could put up me and my team for the night," said the tall driver from the narrow wagon seat. "Come purty far. I'd guess about eighty mile."

Nielson cast a jaundiced eye on the man. No one could have traveled that far in the dilapidated rig drawn by bony horses. But country folk the world over seldom turn away one in need, and it was virtually unknown on the Utah frontier.

"I think the neighbor up the road could pasture your horses," Nielson offered. "I'll go with you."

When the men returned to the house, Mrs. Nielson was ready to serve supper. Nielson looked at his wife, then back to the traveler. "We ain't got much, but if you'd like to share ..."

The man interrupted. "It warms the heart to find such hospitality." Drawing a chair up to the table, he ate and talked at the same time. "I stopped at several places in town, but not a single family was willing to take us in. One day they'll be . . . sorry."

Mrs. Nielson looked uneasily at her husband. Unaccustomed to having strangers in her house, she became nervous. She did not like the man's talk, although she couldn't exactly say why.

After supper, the visitor became more voluble. He spoke of places he'd been all over the world, exotic names such as New York, London, Vienna—places the Nielsons recalled dimly from their geography lessons at country school many years before.

Mrs. Nielson finally decided the man was a liar. She would test him.

"You ever been to Kansas?" she demanded. "I'm from Atchison."

A smile crossed the man's face. "Know it real well. Did you know the Birrells who lived around the corner from the bank? Such a kind family. He had two lovely daughters."

Of course, Mrs. Nielson knew them. Atchison was still a small town. "How . . . how long since you've been there?" she stammered.

"A year and a half," he replied. "You ever know the Walter James family?"

"Their daughter Sue and I were best childhood friends." Mrs. Nielson nodded. "But that was years ago. I lost contact with her."

The man stretched his legs to the fire. "She married Bill Brewer. They got four nice children."

Mrs. Nielson was astounded. Bill Brewer was a mean squirt of a kid, always teasing or mocking someone.

The visitor read her thoughts. "Brewer's a prosperous family man now, real successful. Well liked by everyone."

Suddenly, Mrs. Nielson seemed to lose her breath, bent over and left the room. Her husband explained that the doctors thought she had cancer.

With that the talk ceased, and when Mr. Nielson excused himself the visitor bedded down by the fire. In the morning he did not want breakfast. He seemed somehow chastened, preoccupied. Mrs. Nielson packed him a lunch, and he did agree to take it with him.

"May God bless you always," he said, stepping to the door.
The Nielsons watched him start off down the road. A few minutes later relatives came up that same road, and Mrs. Nielson asked them if they'd met the wagoner with the scrawny team. They said they'd seen no one on the road. There was no other way to go.

In years to come, those families who'd turned their backs on the prophet suffered bad luck while the Nielsons' prosperity increased. But the greatest blessing was the curing of Mrs. Nielson's "cancer." She never endured another pain. And she never did figure out how their visitor knew so much about her hometown. She suspected he'd never been there at all, but how else could he have gained his knowledge of the place?

One day as Mrs. Nielson and her husband talked about the stranger, she exclaimed, "Of course, that's it! He must have been one of *them*!"

Her husband smiled and allowed that he agreed.

John and Isabella Price and their baby son lived in a one-room home in Salt Lake City. John's parents lived with them. When the baby was but a few months old, he became very ill. No remedies seemed to help. Neither did prayers.

Then, late one evening, a stranger knocked at the door and asked for shelter. The man appeared well groomed and wore a gray suit.

Grandpa Price explained that they had no extra beds, but the caller said it didn't matter. He was very weary, he said, and would welcome the opportunity to simply doze by the fire, its heat keeping him warm for the night and the cabin roof sheltering him from the elements.

Grandpa agreed to that. He put another log on the fire, from his own pallet in a dark corner, kept an eye on the sleeping figure. He was determined not to fall asleep lest some harm befell the young family.

Sometime during the night, Grandma Price awakened and saw the stranger sitting at the table. It was covered with a white tablecloth that the family did not own. It was so dazzling white that it hurt her eyes just to look at it. Mesmerized, she watched the man eat bread that seemed to be of the same dazzling white. The Prices never ate white bread.

In the morning, the family offered the visitor breakfast, but he politely declined. Grandpa Price walked him a short ways from the house.

When the old man got back home, he found his grandson cooing and laughing in his crib. He was perfectly fine.

The Prices always believed a Nephite had been sent in answer to their prayers.

On a day in 1944, a man and his wife were traveling by truck across a desolate stretch of highway when they picked up an old man who stood by the roadside. Although he seemed to be somewhat vague about his destination, he was most knowledgeable about current events. He knew a lot about the ongoing World War II and the couple was fascinated by his stories. Then, all of a sudden the man asked to be let out.

"Surely not here," the driver said. "Why, there's no house or building in sight."

The wind was picking up and blowing sand and tumbleweeds across the hood of the truck.

"This is the place," insisted the odd passenger.

Since he couldn't be persuaded to ride on to the next town, the driver let him out.

The old man thanked the couple, then wagged a finger at them.

"On your way back you'll be hauling a dead man. And the war will end in August," he prophesied before disappearing from sight.

The couple soon came upon an automobile accident in which a young man was killed. They hauled the body back to the nearest town. Even though World War II did not end until August of 1945, the man and his wife said the rider had been a Nephite.

In some cases a Nephite happens upon a scene when a life hangs in the balance, as in this case from years ago.

A child not yet in his teens had carried a sack lunch to his father, who owned a flour mill. Once delivered of his obligation, the youngster got to fooling around with the machinery and his hand became caught in a cogwheel. The child's mighty screams brought his father running just at the instant his son pulled his hand loose. The flesh hung in torn and bloody ribbons.

At that moment, a withered, white-bearded man appeared. He grabbed the youngster's wrist and placed a thumb on a vein to stanch the flow of blood. With his other hand, he reached into the flour bin behind him and clapped big handfuls of flour over the injured hand to soak up the blood. Then he turned to the father and instructed him to tear a flour sack into long strips. Working with great skill and care, the old man bound the child's hand with the narrow bands of cloth.

"Don't touch that hand for three weeks," the man instructed before taking his leave.

The boy and his dad went to the mill door, but saw no one in any direction.

The father put his arm around his son. The Good Samaritan had been a Nephite.

The boy's hand was completely healed . . . in three weeks.

A man named Rencher was driving his wagon down a country road when he met an old gentleman. Rencher offered the fellow a ride, and as the two sat together on the high spring seat they talked of the weather and the crops. Eventually, they got to talking about the Book of Mormon. Like many of his neighbors, Rencher attended church, but was not well versed in church doctrine.

The hitchhiker, however, seemed to have a fount of information. He spoke at length about scripture, testimonies, and revelations. Rencher, entranced by the man's knowledge, failed to stop at the neighboring farmhouses as he usually did. He only waved a hand and passed on by.

After some miles, the man asked to be let off; he declined Rencher's invitation to stay overnight at his home. As the man climbed down from the wagon, the skittish horses reared up and, in trying to control them, Rencher lost sight of his companion. He was gone.

Rencher's curiosity was aroused. On his next trip he stopped to ask people along the way if they knew who the man might have been.

"But Brother Rencher," they all pointed out, "there wasn't anyone with you on the wagon seat."

* * *

Are the stories of the Nephites truth or myth? In the end it scarcely matters. The Gentile, or non-Mormon, may doubt their authenticity, but to the devout they offer proof of God's intervention in the affairs of men.

In 1972, distinguished folklorist Jan Harold Brunvand wrote, "... even now, supernaturalism *is* alive and well in Salt Lake City, as elsewhere in Mormon country."

It's likely to remain so for a very long time to come.

Burnley ·

To the casual passerby, the seventy-one-year-old building at Broadway and Pine, in Seattle's Capital Hill district, looks like a typical old office building. But inside, it's far from typical; it harbors a ghost named Burnley, never seen (at least not yet), but often heard.

The South Annex of Seattle Central Community College occupies the building that was, until recently, the home of the Burnley School of Professional Art (renamed the American Institute of Art and now relocated on Elliott Avenue). For over forty years Burnley students and their teachers coexisted, if somewhat uneasily, with an unseen prankster who opened locked doors, rearranged desks, and tramped up and down the rickety wooden stairs. And after the artists moved out, he stayed on in the place he knew as home.

Isbel Trejo-Connor, manager of the college's microcomputer lab on the second floor, says Burnley has a real fondness for women, and never seems to bother the male staff members.

One day in September 1987, Isbel was sitting in the middle of the storage room taking inventory. Suddenly, she was hit on the head by computer disks falling from a shelf. No accident. The shelf was off in a far corner of the room. And she was alone. Several days later, the same thing occurred. Isbel, annoyed, told Burnley to cut it out, that she had work to do. She told a reporter that he hasn't bothered her since.

And who *is* Burnley? Legend has it that he's the spirit of an eighteen-year-old Broadway High School student who was killed during a fight after a basketball game in the one-time gym on the third floor. He either fell or was thrown down a back flight of stairs. No records exist, however, to support the story.

Just why the ghost is named Burnley isn't clear. There doesn't appear to be a connection between the ghost and the art school's founders, Edwin and Elsie Burnley, who taught their first classes there in 1946. From the beginning, students working alone or late at night reported noises in adjacent rooms. Yet whenever they investigated, they could discover no explanation for the noises.

The Burnleys' daughter, Maralyn Blume, assisted them as a receptionist while attending college, and she often found doors, locked at night, mysteriously unlocked the following morning. She could never account for it.

In 1960, Jess Cauthorn, a freelance commercial artist, bought the school from the Burnleys and, unknowingly, inherited the ghost. Cauthorn, a large, amiable man, refused to tell a reporter whether he believes in ghosts, but his daughter, Nan Cooper, says that her father was always frustrated by the inexplicable incidents—lights burning after they'd been turned off, chairs rearranged, and desks overturned—and tended to blame the mischief on the students. Nan said that the students were more willing to risk facing a ghost than the wrath of her father.

Nan, a student at the school from 1973 to 1975 and later a teacher there, is well acquainted with the strange goings-on in the building.

"In the middle of the afternoon you'd be sitting there," she began, "and it was like someone was in the other room doing some paperwork, then walking around. It wasn't that scary ghost stuff; it just seemed like someone was there. And I'd always make sure the front door was locked because sometimes you get weird people off the street, just wanting to go to the bathroom."

Nan learned to shrug off the footsteps, but on one occasion she was badly frightened. Hearing distinct, measured footfalls, "heel, toe, heel, toe" coming close, she said, "I just grabbed my purse, flipped off the lights, and went tearing down the stairs three at a time."

Mary Renick, a former student and part-time office employee, understood that feeling. She was taking down an art display late one night when she heard someone walking down the second-floor hallway. She looked out and the footsteps went right past her! She flew down the stairs and out the building. From then on she wore a cross on her necklace.

The footsteps were not limited to one part of the building, Nan Cooper emphasized. But "there was just always somebody there, just one person, not a crowd." Trash cans were sometimes dumped out, desk drawers thrown open, and sheets of neatly stacked papers found scrunched into balls. Oddly, nothing was ever missing. The incidents happened year-round, but would come in spurts.

No one, except possibly a student named Anita, ever actually saw these things happening. Anita was at her desk one day and saw her X-Acto knife and markers roll across the desktop.

According to Ms. Cooper, almost every janitor who ever worked at the school has at least one story to tell. Her favorite concerns a former janitor and student at the school, who is now an art director in California.

She remembers one incident in particular:

"He'd come in early on a dark winter morning just to sweep up a bit. In order to get the light on you have to go into this real tiny room on the top floor and flip the main switch before you go to the individual rooms. He had gone up there one morning and walked into a dark classroom just to drop his stuff off. As he was going back to turn on the lights he heard this crash and he looked back into the room and saw that three or four desks in the middle row had just flipped over, all askew, chairs overturned. . . ." Nan said the fellow swore the crash had come from inside the room.

Another student-janitor named Mike was working late one night in 1981. As he walked down the hallway to put his bucket and mop away in a storage area inside the men's room, he noticed that the door to that bathroom was just closing. No one was supposed to be in the building. Mike cautiously went into the bathroom and pushed open the doors of the stalls with the mop handle. No one was there. He told the story in the morning to the rest of the staff. Nan Cooper recalled that "it kind of freaked him out." She said the ladies' room too was a place where "the vibes were strong."

And it wasn't only the students and staff who felt that there was something wrong with the building. Visitors often complained of uneasiness or a sudden coldness.

Always there was the unexpressed fear that someone, at some time, might be in danger, but only one incident of physical contact was reported to school officials.

A woman telephoned Jess Cauthorn one night to say that she'd been standing in front of a window on the top floor when she felt something push her from behind. The low windowsill was at the level of her knees. She wheeled around, but saw no one.

The incident that no one has ever forgotten has been dubbed "The Night the Platform Moved."

A five-foot platform on which models posed was always kept in a corner of an upstairs room. One weekend night, the student who had just finished repainting it was downstairs relaxing and eating a hamburger in the locked and empty building. Suddenly, he heard a tremendous crash right over his head. He dashed upstairs and found the big model stand in the opposite corner of the room. How had it gotten there? To this day it remains a mystery.

Jess Cauthorn was a logical man who tried to find answers to the puzzling phenomena in his building. He thought someone *must* be gaining access to the school, and he had the locks changed. It made no difference.

Next, he installed a silent alarm system that alerted a private protection agency should a door or window be opened, or any disturbance trigger the electronic eyes. The system was something of a fiasco. Every alarm turned out to be a false one. The company made no charge for the first false alarm, but each succeeding call cost the school forty-five dollars if security guards were sent out to check.

The alarms kept coming in. Cauthorn finally decided to investigate the school himself whenever the security company called him to say the alarm had gone off. The system was costing him far more than he'd ever anticipated. But he soon tired of being awakened at 2:00 A.M., getting dressed, and driving the thirty miles from his home to the school. He suggested that his daughter be called instead. Nan Cooper lived in an apartment only a few blocks from the school and had a set of keys.

The calls continued—at eleven-thirty, at two, and at four in the morning. Nan always took her boyfriend with her on these middle-of-the-night forays. "We'd take my number-three-iron golf club," she said, "open the door and deactivate the alarm. No one was ever in the place. All the circuits were connected and the doors were locked. We just couldn't figure out what triggered the alarm." Neither could the company that installed the system. They rechecked the wiring and found all connections were in place. Everything, in other words, was in perfect working order.

Sometimes two months would pass without a false alarm, then the phone would ring early in the morning. "At that time of night I knew who it was," she said. "I got to know the guy who worked nights for the company. It became a real joke and he'd start laughing and say 'Okay, what do you want us to do?' and I'd say to just forget it. Nobody ever broke in."

The art school moved out in 1986 and the building was gutted and remodeled. When Nan Cooper heard that supernatural activities were still going on, she was somewhat surprised. "Now there's tinted glass, miniblinds, elevators, and nothing to rattle. You know it'd be a real boring place for a ghost."

Apparently Burnley doesn't agree.

The Tower Ghost

The two Swedish stonemasons neither spoke nor understood English. But they understood their ancient craft well, and, as immigrants, were glad to have found well-paying work. St. Mark's Episcopal Church in Cheyenne would be the most beautiful structure they had ever built, with a magnificent round tower and steeple.

The original church, built in 1868, was the first in Wyoming. But now, in 1886, the congregation wanted a more imposing house of worship, a replica of the British church celebrated in Thomas Gray's poem "Elegy Written in a Country Churchyard."

The Swedes worked well together. From dawn to dusk one operated the horse-drawn hoist on the ground, lifting the precut stones to the other man, who cemented each stone in place. They had already sunk a foundation wall fifteen feet deep to support the massive weight of the bell tower. The walls of the tower would be four feet thick at the base, tapering gradually as the tower grew in height. The work was slow and painstaking, and the rector, Dr. George C. Rafter, asked his parishioners not to distract the men by watching them at work.

One day Dr. Rafter stopped by to see if his men needed anything, possibly more blocks or cement for that day. Only one man was on duty and he seemed highly agitated. Without look-ing up at the rector, he muttered that his partner had taken sick and been unable to report to work.

Dr. Rafter went on about his errands, only to learn the next day that neither workman had appeared. Their landlady said that one of the masons rushed into the house, gathered up the few be-longings of both men and fled. Inquiries were made all over the city, but the Swedes had vanished.

Because American stonemasons lacked the skills at that time to complete the tower, workmen roofed over the uncompleted tower, thus making a study for Dr. Rafter.

In time Dr. Rafter moved on to another church, and his succes-sor was delighted to inherit the quiet, private study. Except that it wasn't quiet. The new rector began hearing hammering sounds in the walls and muffled voices from the ceiling. The attic was checked, but no person or animal was ever found. In 1904, the uneasy clergyman resigned, and the study was permanently sealed off. Sometime later the room was opened up and a new pipe organ installed there.

The congregation, however, was displeased with the uncom-pleted church, and in 1927 workmen were summoned to finish the bell tower. Though plans for a soaring steeple were aban-doned, the round tower rose another sixty feet. Eleven carillons, weighing twenty tons, were installed. But the work did not pro-ceed smoothly. There were arguments and bitter feelings. Some men said the tower was haunted. They heard faint hammering beating against newly laid walls; others heard voices whose words they couldn't distinguish, and still others, hearing nothing unusual, called their fellow workers "crazy." Several times work ceased as angry workmen walked off the job.

When the foreman was no longer able to keep construction go-ing, he appealed to Father Charles Bennett, rector of St. Mark's at that time. Father Bennett was a quiet, thoughtful man who never made a hasty decision.

He didn't believe in ghosts, but he believed in the sincerity of the foremen.

"You think the ghost is a friendly one?" he asked.

The foreman nodded. "The older men tell many strange tales, and sometimes I see the fear in their eyes." He paused. "You see, sir, they believe that the ghost would be happy having its own private room."

Father Bennett was incredulous, but tried not to show it. After a long moment, he said, "All right. Tell your men to proceed."

The private room then built in the tower would have suited the most discerning ghost. Light streaming through the Gothic windows warmed an inlaid wooden floor. A chandelier, hung from the hand-patted plaster ceiling, was often seen burning at night. The room could be reached by a spiral stairway accessible only from a private entrance in the basement. It led to no other room.

Of course after this the haunted tower was no longer a secret. Parishioners and townspeople alike knew the room had been built for a ghost. Churchgoers claimed to hear voices, and although the words were usually jumbled, one sentence came through clearly: "There's a body in the wall." Some members were so frightened that they transferred their memberships to other churches.

The mystery was finally solved in 1966 when the Reverend Eugene Todd, then rector of St. Mark's, was called to a nursing home in Denver where a very old man he had never met wanted to talk to him. The rector was extremely busy with church affairs, but the urgency of the message impelled him to go.

The old man was the surviving Swedish stonemason. He told an incredible story. When he was young, he said, he had worked with a fellow mason on the bell tower for St. Mark's church. The Swede said that one day his partner fell from the tower and was killed instantly when he struck the basement floor. Both men were illegal immigrants and the survivor, fearing deportation or possibly charges of murder, stuffed his partner's body in an unfinished section of the wall, bending it to conform to its curvature. He slathered a layer of cement over the corpse before setting the stones in place over the remains.

The old man sighed and leaned back against his pillows. "I left Cheyenne right off, and went to South America." But now his dying time had come, he said, and he wanted to go back to the United States "to set the record straight." He did not know why or how he had been taken to the Denver nursing home.

Much later, Brad Hamilton, a reporter for the *Wyoming State Tribune*, interviewed Father Todd. Did the minister believe in ghosts?

"No, I do not. But this one I do," he said.

"Why?" Hamilton asked.

"You just come down any evening, let me lock you in the bell tower, then tell me what you think the next morning."

The reporter declined the offer.

In 1979 the bell tower was opened for public tours, an expectedly popular Halloween event. Throngs of residents climbed the eighty-five-foot spiral stairway to the ghost's quarters, laughing and joking about the ghost "snatching" them. Only the hardiest continued their journey up another flight of stairs that led to the carillon room, from which the ghost was said to speak.

Several years later, a Cheyenne radio station invited Ms. Lou Wright, a popular Denver psychic, to spend Halloween night broadcasting from the tower. A deejay would accompany her. Lou figured the program was planned to boost the station's ratings, but no matter. It sounded like fun, and since her expenses would be paid, she agreed to do it. She could not have known the horror that awaited her.

Lou and the deejay met Father Todd at the church, and as the three ascended the stairway to the tower, Lou was overcome with dread. When she mentioned it to the rector he handed her an article about the stonemason buried in the wall. Lou had known nothing of the history of the church.

Soon she felt the presence of a second spirit, this one not nearly so frightening. Who was he? An elderly, white-haired man who walked with a cane, she said. Father Todd told writer Debra M. Munn that the psychic had described the former rector, George Rafter, "exactly as he was. That's surprised me, since she had no way of knowing about him."

Lou and her companion settled into the tower room and Father Todd left, carefully locking all the church doors behind him—to prevent any corporeal entity from entering the building.

The deejay set up his equipment, turned on the transmitter apparatus and Lou, looking out a window, began to describe what she "saw": little balls of white light flitting among the gravestones of the church cemetery far below. She didn't know if they were supernatural or not. At any rate, this would be an interesting evening, Lou thought, and certainly a novel one. Never before had she spent a night in the church tower.

But then, her fear returned. Rows of tiny blue lights "climbed" the stairway to the tower, and in the room itself a slimy substance began oozing from the baseboards. Suddenly, the carillon bells began to ring. Above the din a man's rough voice shouted, "Get out while you still have your mind!"

The deejay broadcast an appeal for help and fortunately his request was not dismissed as a prank. Within fifteen minutes Father Todd and the manager of the radio station arrived and escorted the frightened pair from the church.

Twenty minutes later the bells rang again. Police searched the carillon room and found no evidence of human intervention. The floor was white with dust. Meanwhile, a newspaper reporter at the scene spotted a man sitting in a pew and went to question him. The man vanished. Father Rafter?

Although Lou Wright feels that the spirits were not necessarily evil, but only upset at having their peace disturbed, she vows never to broadcast again from a haunted building. And because of the notoriety occasioned by her visit, the tours of St. Mark's have been discontinued.

Father Todd takes a sanguine attitude toward the phenomena. He believes that his beautiful church is filled with the spirits of many deceased parishioners—men, women and children—and he hopes one day to join them.

Meanwhile, he has been asked if tests would ever be made to determine the location of the stonemason's body. He shakes his head. "That tower ghost . . . has a private chamber suite . . . he can and does play the carillon whenever he wishes."

Most ghosts never have it so good.

CANADA

The Portrait

In December 1965, artist Teresa Montgomery and her husband, Charles, moved into a stately twelve-room house in the Fraser Valley community of Chilliwack. Although the place had been used at one time as a boardinghouse, few major repairs were necessary. Cosmetic improvements alone would certainly go far in restoring the house to its earlier grandeur. The couple were fortunate to have found a house with such potential, and at a reasonable price, no less.

The story of what transpired in the Montgomery's house was one of the most widely reported ghost stories in the British Columbia press of the 1960s. This is what happened to these surprised homeowners.

One afternoon while Teresa worked in the kitchen, she heard drawers opening and closing in an upstairs room. She was alone in the house. Dashing up the stairway, she threw open the doors to all the rooms. In an unused bedroom, she found an old chest that had come with the house, looking as if it had been ransacked; some drawers were partly open, and others were opened wide and jarred off their tracks. An iron bedstead, also left behind by the previous owners, sat in the middle of the floor.

Teresa recalled seeing it against one wall on the day they'd moved in. The chest and the bed were the only furniture in the room.

Teresa didn't tell her husband, but as the days passed she became increasingly nervous in the huge house. Then came the frightening dreams in which she saw a woman lying on the hallway floor. The figure wore a red dress with a pattern of yellow flowers. "She is terrified," Teresa told a reporter.

The nightmares were making her ill. When her husband asked what was the matter, she said she must have become overly tired by the move. She continued to unpack trunks and boxes, arrange furniture, and hang pictures, but took little pleasure in the work. She cooked meals for Charles, but ate sparingly herself. Her husband wasn't overly concerned. He had lived long enough with his wife to recognize the artist's moods. He assumed she had been hard at work on some paintings, and on those occasions little else mattered. She disliked talking about her work, so Charles never asked.

Then, one morning in her studio, Teresa sat down at her easel to paint a portrait of the woman she'd seen in her dreams. Perhaps in this way she could rid herself of the ghastly dream. But something took control of the brush in her hand. Although she tried to paint the portrait of a woman, the face became that of a man—a man with strong, dark, virile features.

Nothing like this had ever happened to the artist before. Was she losing her talent? Her mind? Fright drove her from the studio that afternoon.

The next day Teresa found the portrait she'd left on the easel had changed. The man's dark eyes had become menacing, and deep shadows concealed one side of his face. Each morning thereafter Teresa would find the portrait altered in some way. She knew then that she would never be able to paint again, at least not in *this* house.

Then late one night a slight noise sent Teresa again into the unused bedroom. As she peered through the door, a dim light appeared in a window and in the center of the light she glimpsed a woman's face. Although the features were somewhat indistinct, Teresa felt certain that this was the woman in her nightmares. This was the ghost who haunted her house.

Soon after the actual sighting of the mysterious woman, other phenomena developed. The front door began to open and close by itself. Footfalls were heard on the stairs when no one was there, and sounds of heavy breathing came from empty rooms.

As Teresa became acquainted with her neighbors, they told her tales about her house—perhaps more than she wanted to hear. One account had it that a woman had ben murdered in the house and her body cremated in the chimney. Another story was of a man who'd committed suicide in the house a decade earlier. He was said to have occupied the empty room. The worried home-owner wondered if that might account for the heavy breathing she had heard. No one seemed to know if there'd been any connection between the two people, or, indeed, if either story had any basis in fact.

However, the previous owners, Rebecca and Jackson Perkins, told the Montgomerys that an old man living in the house *had* committed suicide, but he drowned himself in a slough behind the house. Mr. and Mrs. Perkins noted that they'd experienced nothing unusual during the four years they had lived in the house, and dismissed the rumors of ghost business as "baloney."

By spring the media got wind of the strange goings-on in Chilliwack. Teresa eagerly accepted all requests by reporters and photographers to tour the house, and she took special pains to show them the four-by-six-foot portrait that she claimed was changing daily. She said the dark side of the picture had lightened, the outline of a cheek appeared, and a thin moustache was now visible.

One night during the last week of May 1966, Jess Odam, a staff reporter for the *Vancouver Sun*, and Ken Oakes, a *Sun* photographer, visited the house. They kept vigil in the unused bedroom, which was lit by one candle on the chest. A friend of Teresa Montgomery who did not wish to be identified sat with the two men. Teresa was in the kitchen preparing sandwiches.

At 12:25 A.M., Odam reported that he thought he heard a footstep out in the hallway. The friend said she'd heard a "sliding sound." Oakes, seated farthest from the doorway, heard nothing.

Moments later when Teresa came up the stairs with the tray of sandwiches, she discovered a piece of linoleum lying on the hallway floor. She took it into the room and showed her guests the place where it had been tacked to the wall. She'd seen it there on the day she and her husband had moved in and was certain that it was in place when the little group arrived.

Odam wrote, "We saw no ghost; we heard no ghost . . . or did we?"

The following week, at Teresa's request, Odam returned to the house to investigate a small turret at the corner of the building. Teresa had dreamed that the ghost lady "lived" in there. Perhaps the turret held a clue as to the woman's identity and her fate. Before Odam reached the house, Teresa had already broken an opening into the turret by removing some attic paneling. But fearing spiders, she dared not go in.

Odam armed himself with a flashlight and squeezed into the tiny space. Lying on his stomach, he swung the flashlight slowly in all directions. Nothing. Nothing but insulation material that had crumbled over the years and now littered the small floor. When Teresa saw it she said it looked similar to the white specks she'd seen in her dreams.

Shortly after Odam's visit, a former occupant telephoned the Montgomerys to report that there were secret chutes running from the top of the house to the bottom. For what purpose the caller did not know. Teresa suspected it was a prank call, but there were so many questions without answers that she scheduled a séance.

A hypnotist and a clairvoyant met at the house on an afternoon in June. Teresa had moved a table and chairs into the empty bedroom. As the men seated themselves, she pulled down the room-darkening shades at the windows and lit a candle in the center of the table. Charles Montgomery was posted in the front yard to keep sightseers away. (The newspaper articles had attracted some unwanted attention.)

"Is there anyone here?" asked the clairvoyant. "You may come forth now, please."

Silence.

The clairvoyant raised his voice. "We are here only to help you."

Teresa stared so intently at the candle that she saw multiple images of the flame.

"Do not fear us," said the hypnotist. "We bring you no harm."

There were no sounds save the rhythmic breathing of the three persons at the table.

The clairvoyant folded his hands together. "We implore you to go to the light. You are dead and on this earth plane there is nothing more for you. In the kingdom of light others will help you."

Teresa thought that one window shade rippled at the sill, but she couldn't be certain.

As the summer days stretched into weeks and the weeks into months, hundreds of people besieged the homeowners, all wanting tours of the "spook" house. Children told their wide-eyed classmates that caskets floated from room to room and skeletons rattled up and down the staircase. All nonsense, of course.

The Montgomerys finally posted a NO SIGHTSEERS sign on the door, but it had no effect. In one week alone two hundred cars a day disgorged noisy ghost hunters, and on one Sunday seven hundred people broke the front steps trying to gain entry to the house. Teresa, exhausted from the turbulent publicity, refused to admit anyone unless they had written her a letter first. And letters were arriving daily from all parts of Canada.

Charles Montgomery resented the flood of letters and the unruly strangers who banged at the door and peeked in the windows at all hours of the day and night. There could be only one solution. The couple would charge admission to tour their home! Surely anyone wishing to see a house "infested" with ghosts would be willing to pay for the privilege.

But Teresa Montgomery didn't reckon on the trouble she would have getting a trade license to operate a "haunted house."

Chilliwack's acting mayor, Al Holden, said that if the council granted her request then the entire neighborhood would have to be rezoned from residential to commercial. Alderman Bill Nickel said he felt Mrs. Montgomery only wanted to exploit the free publicity she'd received about her claims that ghosts were in her house.

One day Teresa and a friend discovered that the portrait was fading and also *shrinking* in size. They measured it to confirm their suspicions and wondered how such a feat could be accomplished.

Dr. Geoffrey Riddehough, a lecturer in classics at the University of British Columbia and a member of the Psychical Research Society of England, was invited to study the portrait. He came to no conclusions, other than to remark that there are some things happening in the world for which people have no explanation.

Eventually, Teresa grew sick of the portrait and threatened to get rid of it. She did. The Pacific National Exhibition displayed it for a while, and in 1973 it became the property of a Vancouver radio station. Press accounts do not mention the picture's condition at that time.

Were the accounts of the Chilliwack haunting genuine? That question is impossible to answer. The local journalist who first broke the story said Mrs. Montgomery told her the painting would put the little town on the map. That it certainly did. But the reporter spent many hours and days in the house and, according to an interview with her, "never saw anything or heard anything to suggest the place was haunted."

In 1972 the Montgomerys sold the house and moved to Vancouver Island to enjoy a more tranquil life in a house presumably free of unwanted guests.

The new owner stayed in the mansion for barely a year. He said that he and his family were moving for personal reasons. He did not elaborate. The house sold for $23,000 to a young Chilliwack couple who intended to renovate it and raise a family there. The new buyers knew the ghost legend, but didn't think much of it.

A Chilliwack real estate agent who handled the sale said the transaction was not that difficult, despite the house's history.

"It used to be that selling a haunted house was a real estate man's nightmare," he told a Canadian Press reporter. "But not anymore. Today, haunted houses seem to attract more interest than those that are not. . . ."

If the new owners ever did start seeing strange sights and hearing unusual noises in their notorious home, they had only to call the agent for reassurance that no one else shared their home. You see, the Realtor did not believe in ghosts.

NOTE: Certain names in this story have been changed.

Mysterious Ontario

A young man with dark hair who wants to live with his old friends ... the ghost whose likeness was immortalized in a gargoyle's face ... a wandering singer in Yorkville ... and a famous house whose spirits may be of the fictional variety. Ghosts and haunted places have been reported for many decades in Ontario Province and its largest city, Toronto.

An Unwanted Visitor

A pleasant avenue in suburban Toronto would seem an unlikely place to find the supernatural, but don't tell that to one young couple who moved into the basement apartment of a neat brick home on just such a boulevard several years ago.

The series of events that inexplicably plagued the pair were serious enough to warrant a "dehaunting" by Ian Currie and Carole Davis, two Canadian investigators of the paranormal.

Twenty-year-old Rob, his wife Cindy, nineteen, and their infant son had been in their new apartment barely a month when a growling sound coming from their child's room startled them awake late one night. The couple found the tyke standing up in bed staring at the wall. He seemed scared about something, his mother said. The source of the menacing growl remained a puzzlement.

Over the next few weeks, the child experienced further episodes of sudden crying and screaming. The couple were at a loss to explain his fearful outbursts.

Other freakish occurrences scared Rob and Cindy. A coffeemaker spurted hot water for no apparent reason, a window slammed shut on a still night, and, most incredible of all, a glass full of milk glided halfway across a table as the couple looked on in amazement. When a friend stayed overnight in the baby's room, she told Cindy about being awakened by a breeze across her face, and of seeing a pallid, yellow light shining down from above.

The couple found out about Ian Currie, an author and former professor, and Carole Davis, a psychic who claimed to have helped police in Canada and the United States. Their little apartment needed, the parents decided, a professional ghost-cleansing.

Currie and Davis claimed to have dehaunted nearly sixty homes at the rate of $250 Canadian per house. "Satisfaction guaranteed," Currie told newspaper reporter Gerald Volgenau.

Davis was in the apartment only a short while when she pronounced it definitely haunted. But the ghost was not an evil presence, "just a poor person in distress," she said. Further, she sensed the presence was that of a dark-haired young man killed in a traffic accident.

Psychic Davis went into a trance with Currie at her side. Within minutes, she was speaking for the ghost—of the driving rain, of the darkness and sudden headlights, of the trouble he had caused for his loved ones, and of his desire to go home. Meanwhile, Ian Currie was talking soothingly to his unseen listener, telling him that he was dead, that the accident was not his fault. He should "go into the light," Currie insisted.

Soon the psychic was quiet, her head jerking slightly as if to clear it of the last vestiges of the visiting spirit.

Cindy was stunned at the scene. She had known just such a man, a young acquaintance who had been drinking one night and stumbled in front of an oncoming car during a rainstorm. He was killed instantly.

It can only be surmised that his ghost had for some reason attached itself to the young couple. But now he was gone, Currie and Davis said. Rob and Cindy were relieved. The apartment was definitely *not* big enough for four.

Ivan the Ghost

No! It just wasn't possible, the surly master stonemason screamed, throwing down his chisel and hammer. His friend Sergei Ilyitch backed away. Maybe this hadn't been such a good idea, he thought. Sergei had only wanted to be helpful by pointing out that Ivan Reznikoff's face was being carved in a gargoyle on the central facade of University College. Another mason, Paul Diabolos, was the culprit. To him it was a big joke, but to Ivan the thought of *his* face on that of a grotesque and ugly statue was outrageous.

And now the insult had turned to rage. Sergei had just added the news that Diabolos was after Ivan's girlfriend, Susie.

"If you do not believe me," Sergei stammered as he edged away, fearful of the muscular Russian's temper, "come back tonight and wait at the Arcade. That's where they meet. You will see."

To this Ivan agreed. But until nightfall, he would start exacting his own revenge—the gargoyle upon which he, himself, was working would have a new feature . . . the face of the miscreant Diabolos!

The year was 1858. The Toronto architects Cumberland and Storm had the commission to design and build University College at the University of Toronto. When they had advertised for workmen, a squat, heavily muscled, bearded Russian named Ivan Reznikoff was among the applicants. He showed the architects his carvings. They were pleased with his work and hired him to create some of the gargoyles on the central facade.

Not a great deal was, or is, known about Reznikoff. He was born in Russia sometime in the early nineteenth century and had shown up in Canada in the mid-1840s. One version of his life claims he worked for Messrs. Cumberland and Storm on projects even before University College. He told them he had carved statues in cities all across Europe and worked for a while in Britain, bragging that he had carvings on buildings around Piccadilly Circus.

Though he was a good worker, Reznikoff was a sullen, solitary figure with few close friends. His disdain for human contact was the cause of his global wanderlust. Carving was his only pleasure, especially cutting stone into the gremlins and gargoyles and other vermin of the night. Some said the nightmares that plagued him led to his most creative work.

Reznikoff did not seek, nor was there extended to him, the friendship of others. Sergei Ilyitch, a fellow Russian émigré, was the only one in whom Reznikoff ever confided. So Ilyitch felt an obligation to point out that Paul Diabolos's interest in the Russian's girlfriend. The girl's last name isn't known, nor is there any indication of how or why the gruff Russian and the Canadian girl got together, but Diabolos must have thought it great sport to steal the only woman in whom Reznikoff showed an interest, albeit an affection she did not save for him alone.

As night fell, Reznikoff hid in the arcade of the building. A few minutes later, Diabolos and Susie came into view, hand-in-hand and laughing gaily. It was all too much for Reznikoff. He charged at Diabolos, his mason's axe held high above his head. He swung a mighty blow, but Diabolos ducked and Reznikoff's axe struck an oaken door. The deep gash remains visible to this day.

Diabolos ran up the stairs of the central tower. He crouched in a dark corner, drew a small dagger from his waistband and waited. When the mad Russian appeared, Diabolos leaped out and plunged the knife into his attacker's heart. He pushed Reznikoff's corpse down the twelve-story, unfinished central tower well.

During the 1860s, 1870s, and 1880s, students, faculty, and visitors at the university sometimes reported seeing a dark figure wearing a conical hat suddenly appear in the vicinity of the tower. The story was told about how Reznikoff had died. Others said it was just a legend, until . . .

A fire swept through University College in 1890. In the rubble, searchers found a skull and bones and a silver buckle—at the bottom of the tower's well. Just where Ivan Reznikoff was said to have been deposited. His remains were reburied in a corner of the quadrangle.

Does Ivan Reznikoff still haunt University College? Any strange noise in the building is attributed to Reznikoff, but there have been no recent, verified reports. Staff and students treat the legend with a certain lighthearted air. A pub in the building's basement was even named after him. But, still, if you linger long enough beneath one of the Reznikoff gargoyles on a moonlit night . . . anything is possible.

The ROM

On Queen's Park Crescent, the Royal Ontario Museum may have two old ghosts in addition to its eclectic collection of Canadiana.

The better known of the pair may be the ghost of the museum's former director, Dr. Charles Currelly, who was eighty-two when he died in 1957. He was director of the museum for thirty-two years, from 1914 until his retirement in 1946.

Dr. Currelly isn't a frightening specter at all, just peculiarly dressed. He wears a nightshirt and cap as he scurries down the corridor. Precisely why he is dressed this way, or the reason for his haste, is not known.

A little curly-haired blond girl of about eight was seen in the planetarium section of the museum in the late 1970s. She wore a starched white dress and looked very unhappy, according to one museum staff member. Unfortunately, as with many ghosts, no one knew her name or the nature of her distress.

Yorkville Apparitions

Whenever old houses are converted to more modern uses, say offices or trendy shops, incorporeal residents of those selfsame dwellings can put a chill into any business climate. Such was the case in two circa-1900 Yorkville homes.

A house on Hazelton Avenue was remodeled into offices for a music production company, but that didn't stop the vocalizings of a female ghost. A company executive working late heard the singing while locking up for the night. He said it was quite a "beautiful" sound. So far as is known no attempt was made to sign her to a contract.

A psychic who worked in the house some years ago said it may have been a woman who lived there during World War II, and was still waiting for her husband to return. The woman was once seen walking down a second-floor hallway, and thence through a wall and front window.

Another man claimed the alarm system, which used motion detectors and infrared light beams, was always going off. The police eventually refused to respond to any alarms at the house, he said.

The people who built a house on Roxborough Street may be still looking after the place. According to reports from 1986, the woman who then ran a business there said her cat always acted strangely in the house. A medium was consulted, and she said there were several friendly ghosts present. To a spirit, they were happy with what the woman was doing with their old house, the medium said, and only wanted to protect what had been theirs in life.

Mackenzie House

Did the ghost of Isabel Mackenzie really slap the caretaker at the historic William Lyon Mackenzie House?

The most often-told ghost story in Toronto concerns the mansion at 82 Bond Street where the Canadian statesman and Toronto's first mayor lived from 1859 until his death in 1861. He died an ill-tempered and disillusioned old man. Mackenzie himself was supposedly seen and heard hanging about his former home, running the hand-operated Washington flatbed printing press and playing the pump organ. But it is his wife, Isabel, who has been the subject of the most frequent supernatural tales. Are they true?

"The Mackenzie House is not haunted," Mrs. E. M. Drake, a curatorial assistant at Mackenzie House, said. "Such stories did circulate during the 1950s, but there have been absolutely no such manifestations since the Toronto Historical Board assumed management of the house in 1960. Despite this, a public perception that we are haunted does continue to persist, reinforced each Halloween by our local media, who conveniently ignore our assurances and the fact that the house was exorcised in 1960."

Exorcised?

The simple fact that it was deemed necessary to conduct such a religious ceremony may of itself suggest that there was more to the haunting than anyone cares to admit. And that's certainly not surprising considering the disputatious life of William Lyon Mackenzie.

A native of Dundee, Scotland, Mackenzie emigrated to Canada in 1820 at the age of twenty-five. With a partner, Mackenzie was soon in business operating a drug- and book-selling business in York, later the city of Toronto. He married Isabel Baxter, to whom he had become engaged in Scotland, in 1822.

Mackenzie began his career as a journalist in 1824 with the appearance of *The Colonial Advocate* newspaper in Queenston, where he had moved after his marriage. His career as a radical politician and proponent of Canadian self-rule ascended upon his move back to York, the provincial capital, and with his increasingly strident editorials criticizing the "Family Compact," a close-knit group of influential provincial families. His words stung so deeply that in 1826 the sons of some of the prominent families broke into his print shop and wrecked his presses.

The general public, however, rushed to his defense and elected him to a seat in the Assembly of Upper Canada in 1828 as a leader of the radical wing of the Reform Party. His firebrand rhetoric continued to get him into trouble. He was expelled from the Assembly on numerous occasions and finally denied his seat in that body.

His overall popularity remained high, however, and in 1834 he was elected alderman of the new city of Toronto and then mayor, becoming thereby the first chief executive of what is now Canada's largest city.

Mackenzie found the years following fraught with rejection and disillusionment. He was defeated for reelection in 1836, along with other members of the Reform Party.

It was at this point in his stormy career that Mackenzie began to advocate open rebellion against the government, which he criticized as unresponsive and unrepresentative. Not content to use words alone, he led seven hundred men in the ill-fated December 1837 coup attempt. He was just able to flee with his supporters to Navy Island in the Niagara River where he announced a provisional government that was rejected by Canadian, United States, and British authorities.

The United States tried and convicted Mackenzie of treason in 1839. Eventually the Canadian government pardoned Mackenzie, and the rebels and he returned home. He served seven more years in the Legislative Assembly and established a new newspaper, *Mackenzie's Weekly Message*. He published it until 1860.

His final years were full of bitterness over his failed political ambitions and his financial difficulties. His friends raised funds to purchase the house on Bond Street, and Mackenzie lived there from 1859 until he died on August 28, 1861.

The exorcism that reportedly took place in 1960 was probably aimed at persuading William's wife, Isabel, to leave the premises. Following her death in 1873, there were periodic reports in the press claiming Mrs. Mackenzie's ghost was seen marching down the stairs and out the front door. Those stories, of course, preceded the story of her slapping the caretaker, which has variously been reported as having occurred sometime in the 1950s or early 1960s. Her ghost was also said to have jealously guarded the kitchen. Employees said they, too, were sometimes slapped by nothing they could see when they came into the kitchen from the back door.

Sources say her ghost was finally put to rest when a minister was summoned by Col. Charles Lindsey, the Mackenzies' grandson. The unnamed minister held a service during which he asked Mrs. Mackenzie's ghost to relocate somewhere else.

The media continue to include the Mackenzie House on their

annual Halloween Toronto "ghost tour," but it would seem that its days of being haunted are over. At least for now.

The Tombstone

Mike Cino's demolition firm had nearly finished ripping apart the second floor of the old building they'd been hired to raze in Hamilton during the fall of 1982. The work was progressing smoothly. Nothing untoward or terribly unusual had happened. The workers had found the customary odds and ends and bric-a-brac in the place, but certainly nothing that would set back their timetable.

On this particular day a worker thought he had heard a strange noise from within the building as the machines tore into the structure, but he attributed it to the groans of a well-made house reluctantly giving way to the wrecker's ball.

Then they found the tombstone.

Discovered secreted in a wall of the second floor, the stone bore the chiseled words OUR BABY at the top. Below, two names were still clearly discernible: *Martha Louise, 1888;* and *Emma Grace, Nov. 9, 1879.*

No one knew who the little children might have been, or why they died. Nor could Mike Cino guess why the stone was placed where it was found, other than the possibility that it might have been used to prop up the wall.

The discovery, however, was critical for helping to solve an eleven-year-old mystery: the possible cause of frightening visits from a ghost witnessed by two former residents.

Norm Bilotti worked in the composing room of the *Hamilton Spectator* in the early 1970s. He lived in the house with his wife, Sherrie. Their brush with the supernatural came quite unexpectedly, in the middle of the night. Twice.

The first time, Norm jerked awake when his wife screamed at the top of her lungs from the bed next to him. He blinked in the gloomy darkness until he was able to focus on what his wife saw—a human form wearing a long gown hovering above their bed. He couldn't see any face. He had no idea if it was male or female. Only that it was there.

"If she had only seen it herself, I would have thought she was crazy," Norm said in a Canadian Press account of the incident. "If it had only been me, I would have thought I was crazy. But both of us saw it."

The figure vanished when Norm turned on the light.

The second time they knew for *certain* neither was dreaming. Norm saw it first this night, and his cries awoke his wife. A legless woman hovered near them, her eyes protruding grotesquely from her face. And her hair . . . her hair stood on end as if she had stuck her finger in an electrical outlet. She said not a word and then was gone.

Despite the unnerving, middle-of-the-night episodes, the Bilottis had a certain curiosity about the identity of the ghost. They thought a ghost hunter might provide some clues and called Malcolm Bessent, of Rosary Hill College in Buffalo, New York.

Bessent visited the home and immediately sensed a "presence" in the house. "I think something is concealed in this area—what, I don't know," he said, pointing to a particular section of a wall. "I'm being drawn to it very strongly. It's the reason for the manifestation."

The Bilottis never again were visited by the mysterious woman and moved out of the house shortly thereafter. They thought nothing more would ever be heard about the ghost until . . .

. . . Mike Cino's crew began leveling the old house. He wasn't surprised at finding the nineteenth-century tombstone—after all, he had once found a *bomb* in one place—but it was a bit odd that such a marker would be used to shore up a wall.

Norm Bilotti found out about the discovery. It all made sense, and at the same time chilled the very marrow in his bones.

The tombstone was found *directly above* the bedroom in which the couple had seen the ghost. And further, Malcolm Bessent had pointed to nearly the *precise section of the wall* where the stone was discovered. Norm and Sherrie had seen a ghost . . . and it was somehow connected to the tombstone.

The identity of the two children memorialized on the stone was never established. Was it their mother the Bilottis saw? If so, there might be presented here further evidence that a mother takes care of her children—even after death.

Author's Note

Do you have an interesting ghost story to tell, either from personal experience or one based on legend or folklore? If you would like to share your story, write to Michael Norman, c/o Tom Doherty Associates, 175 Fifth Avenue, New York, NY 10010.